A JUST PEACE IN THE MIDEAST:
HOW CAN IT BE ACHIEVED?

First in the fifth series of Rational Debate Seminars
sponsored by the American Enterprise Institute
held at
The Madison Hotel
Washington, D.C.

PETER LISAGOR
Moderator

A JUST PEACE IN THE MIDEAST: HOW CAN IT BE ACHIEVED?

I. L. Kenen
Elmer Berger
Allen Pollack
Christopher Mayhew

RATIONAL DEBATE SEMINARS

American Enterprise Institute
for Public Policy Research
Washington, D.C.

A JUST PEACE IN THE MIDEAST:
HOW CAN IT BE ACHIEVED?

I. L. Kenen
Elmer Berger
Allen Pollack
Christopher Mayhew

Published by

American Enterprise Institute
for Public Policy Research

The four distinguished speakers in this debate agree on two essential points: first, the search for an enduring peace in the Middle East will continue to be long and arduous, and second, failure to reach a settlement could result in a catastrophic confrontation between the Soviet Union and the United States. They disagree sharply, however, on the causes of the conflict, on the measures necessary to resolve it, and on the ingredients of a just peace.

A "Just Peace in the Mideast: How Can It Be Achieved?" represents the first seminar in AEI's fifth rational debate series. The remarks of the four debaters vividly illustrate the formidable problems that have plagued the Middle East story for over two decades.

I. L. Kenen of the American Israel Public Affairs Committee and Professor Allen Pollack of the American Professors for Peace in the Middle East are ardent admirers of Israel and share the view that her survival is important to the United States. Thus, Mr. Kenen asserts that "Israel and America are united by a common commitment to democracy and freedom." And Professor Pollack states that the U.S. . . . . "should support Israel, not for the interests of the Jewish people but because America has vital interests in the Middle East which Israel is protecting."

Both men call for U.S. economic and military aid to Israel in sufficient quantity to enable her to meet what they view as a serious Soviet threat. In Mr. Kenen's opinion, the U.S.S.R. must bear the primary guilt for the continuing tension in the Middle East because "she backs and leads the Arabs on the diplomatic and military fronts as part of her strategy to dominate the Near East and Africa." Professor Pollack agrees, describing the Middle East as "the newest and most volatile front reheating the cold war between East and West," and arguing that the Soviet Union sees a prolonged Arab-Israeli dispute as facilitating the spread of Soviet influence in the area.

Mr. Christopher Mayhew, a labor member of the British Parliament, and Rabbi Elmer Berger, probably the leading Jewish anti-Zionist in the United States, view the Soviet threat in the Middle East from a different perspective. Mr. Mayhew thinks the Soviet Union has furnished assistance to Egypt and the Arab countries reluctantly—"in response to fervent and repeated pleas from Nasser, arising from his inability to defend his own territory and people." He considers the Palestinian question the principal obstacle to a peace settlement. "It is a terrible truth," Mr. Mayhew says, "that the Palestinian Arabs have now been dispersed from Palestine by the Jews much as the Jews were dispersed from Palestine by the Romans, and that their reactions are just as passionate and enduring."

Professor Pollack, on the other hand, maintains that solution of the Palestinian question depends on the goodwill of the Arab and Soviet leaderships. "The Arabs need and want to live in a world of illusion," he says, "maintaining their stance of hatred of Israel and perpetuating their hostility. It is only . . . the actions of the Soviet Union that have enabled the Arabs to continue this policy."

Rabbi Berger is highly critical of Zionist expansionism which, in his view, justifies the Arab fear that Israel will not relinquish territory conquered in 1967 and may even try to seize more. He strongly disputes the Zionist assumption that all Jews, no matter where they live, are Israeli nationals. In his opinion, the establishment of Israel was a mistake in the first place but, nevertheless, the fact of its existence must be reflected in any Mideast peace settlement. In addition, he says, a just settlement must include Israeli recognition of the rights of the Palestinians, internationalization of Jerusalem and a return to the borders outlined in the 1947 U.N. resolution.

While the United States cannot force the Israelis to change their position on these issues, Rabbi Berger says, there are certain steps it can and should take. "Zionism/ Israel's 'Jewish people' nationality is inconsistent with the Constitution of the United States," he says. "We cannot force Israel to surrender it. But we can refuse to permit its application to Americans and we can deny the Zionist state the privilege of subsidizing its 'Jewish people' nationality apparatus with tax deductible American dollars."

Mr. Mayhew, while agreeing with Rabbi Berger that Israeli leaders are expansionist, contends that Israel's "overriding demand is for security." Unfortunately, he says, true security is impossible, as long as Israel remains so aggressive and as long as it continues to occupy Arab territory seized in the 1967 war and to claim exclusive control of Jerusalem. "No country which occupies tens of thousands of square miles of its neighbor's territory (and rules over more than a million of their people with an increasingly heavy hand) can expect to live in peace or indeed deserves to do so." Mr. Mayhew holds that Israeli withdrawal to the pre-1967 borders is a necessary precondition for peace talks, whereas Mr. Kenen finds "nothing rational" in such a demand.

With respect to the role of the Great Powers in producing a settlement, Mr. Kenen and Professor Pollack strongly favor direct Arab-Israeli talks and fear that any Soviet-American attempt to exert excessive pressure on the two sides or to impose a settlement would be inadvisable and, perhaps, counterproductive. More specifically, Mr. Kenen opposes Great Power involvement on the ground that it would "enable the Soviet Union to try to dictate the terms of a settlement and to entrench itself as the dominant power in the region." In contrast, Mr. Mayhew appeals for heavy Soviet-American pressure on both Arabs and Israelis in order to obtain a peace settlement establishing, among other things, a demilitarized border zone manned by U.N. forces.

All four debaters, although uncertain and pessimistic about the future of this situation, recognize the need to continue the search for a just peace. The sharpness of their disagreements and the strength of their convictions in themselves reflect the intensity of the conflict and the difficulties inherent in solving it.

FOREWORD

Since Israel's creation in 1948, the conflict between Arabs and Israelis in the Middle East has been making the headlines. The difficult problems underlying this conflict have plagued all efforts at establishing a workable peace and, at times, have threatened the peace of the world.

This debate brings together four men who are in sharp disagreement over both the issues of this controversy and the conditions necessary to a just peace. They agree only on the urgent need to reach an enduring settlement—and on the fact that such a settlement is not likely to come easily or soon.

"Just Peace in the Mideast: How Can It Be Achieved?" represents the first seminar in AEI's fifth rational debate series. These debates are designed to explore in depth the facts, conflicts and opinions surrounding the important public issues of our time.

September 1971

William J. Baroody
President
American Enterprise Institute
for Public Policy Research

CONTENTS

FIRST LECTURE

I. L. KENEN

I. The Current Crisis

The standstill cease-fire agreement accepted by Egypt, Jordan, and Israel seemed to offer a slim ray of hope for peace. But that ray soon faded out when the Soviet Union and Egypt rushed to build missile sites and moved dozens of missiles into the prohibited zone. They conspired to exploit the breathing spell in order to prepare for a new military or diplomatic showdown when the cease-fire ended—to dictate Israel's surrender and to impose a pro-Arab settlement.

Our State Department has insisted that Egyptian President Nasser wants a peaceful solution—that he does not really want to drive Israel into the sea. But on the very day that Secretary of State Rogers announced his peace initiative, Nasser said:

> The Arab masses know that their strength lies in their unity . . . and unity means the end of imperialism and its collaborators and the liquidation of Israeli aggression and the Zionist entity.

Moreover, as the talks began, the Arabs said once again: no negotiations, no peace treaties, and no surrender of the claims of the Palestinians. That is what they tell their own people. Why do our diplomats always deceive themselves into believing the Arab leaders lie to their people but confide the truth to us?

Within the first few days of the cease-fire, Israel called upon the United States to enforce President Nixon's commitment that a military buildup would not occur. But the United States was slow in acknowledgment, weak in action. Indeed, our government seemed to be more displeased with Israel for the complaint than with the Egyptians for the violation.

The United States was the victim of a hoax, did not want to admit it, and was angry with the fellow victim who refused to accept the growing peril to her survival and who had acted on U.S. representations. And that dereliction raises grave doubts about the credibility of the U.S. commitment. Can Israel rely on any kind of U.S. commitment or guarantee?

Often in the past—in 1948 after the partition decision, in 1951 after the Security Council ordered Egypt to open the canal, and again, in 1967, after Nasser closed the Straits of Tiran—Israel learned that she could not rely on third parties or agencies to enforce and safeguard ephemeral guarantees. This time, Israel insists there must be genuine peace treaties, signed by the parties and obligating them to each other—in indelible, not invisible, ink.

It appears now that the Israelis are facing a peace-at-any-price pressure to make dangerous concessions as in the disastrous rollback of 1957. In one critical

aspect the danger is much worse today than it was in
1957, because now the Russians are massed—with men
and missiles—on Israel's doorstep. The danger which
Israel faces and about which she is trying to alert the
world resembles the crisis our own country faced in
Cuba in 1962.

II. Background: The Role of the Great Powers

It is frequently said that Israel is caught up in the
crossfire of three wars: the war between the Arab states
and herself; the Arab-Arab conflict between the radical
Soviet-supported states and the conservative Western-
oriented states; and the cold war between East and
West, where she finds herself defending the interests
of the free world but without its active support.

The Great Powers compete for influence and prestige
and power. The maldistribution of resources in the
Arab world drives the dispossessed and revolutionary
"have-nots" towards conflict with the "haves." It is a
conflict between states. It is also a conflict inside the
states between the rich and the poor. It is a vast over-
simplification to suggest that our support for Israel has
been the reason for Western setbacks. In the cold war,
the West has been at a disadvantage, not only because
the Russians fight Israel but because we have always
been identified with reactionary rulers and because our
large oil companies have extracted huge profits from
the region, thus exposing America to left-wing attack.

Israel has been imperiled as the Arabs played off

Great Power rivalries. Before World War II, the Arabs flirted with the Nazis, and the British were ready to sacrifice the Jewish national home. Since World War II, the Arabs have tried to blackmail the West by threatening to transfer their allegiance, their oil, and their political and propaganda power to Moscow.

Obviously, Russia must bear primary guilt because she backs and leads the Arabs on the diplomatic and military fronts as part of her strategy to dominate the Near East and Africa. She is unscrupulous in her harassment of Israel, cynical in her deception of Washington.

But Washington and London also have much to answer for. Western support for Israel has been a frail reed, swaying weakly before every Arab threat, succumbing to every Arab blackmail. The British reneged on their commitment and responsibility under the Balfour Declaration and the League of Nations Mandate.

And, as for the United States, our policy has been equivocal, erratic, and inconsistent for a quarter of a century. We have raised expectations in Arab capitals that the United States might ultimately abandon Israel.

In 1947, the UN Special Committee on Palestine recommended partition offering self-rule to both the Jews and the Arabs in separate states. The Arabs rejected the compromise; the Jews reluctantly agreed. The UN General Assembly voted for it. President Truman endorsed the concept of partition, despite the hostility of the Departments of State and Defense and the lobbying of oil and missionary interests. The partition proposal was to be implemented by a special Palestine commission. Obstruction would constitute a breach of the peace enabling the Security Council to take appropriate action.

All UN debate and documents confirm that the Arab states resisted implementation. The partition commission never went to Palestine.

In 1948, we tried to set aside the UN partition resolution. In 1949, we again brought pressure on Israel to make territorial concessions to the Arabs, even threatening to reconsider U.S. relations with Israel. In 1956, the United States joined with the Soviet Union in forcing Israel to withdraw to the 1949 armistice lines without requiring the Arab states to renounce belligerence and to enter into peace treaties with Israel.

While we gave generous economic assistance to both Israel and the Arab states, we repeatedly refused Israel's requests for arms, even after the Soviet Union began arming the Arab states. We detoured her to other countries. In lieu of arms we offered guarantees—the Tripartite Declaration, the Middle East Eisenhower Doctrine, a succession of promises and commitments from Presidents Eisenhower, Kennedy, Johnson, and Nixon. But these commitments all vanished like mirages whenever crises came close.

And often over the years we seemed to be in competition with the Soviet Union for the favor of the Arab states and certain charismatic Arab leaders like

President Nasser of Egypt. Today, a major objective
of our policy seems to be the restoration of diplomatic
relations with Nasser—as well as economic aid—which
explains our diffidence in calling him to account for
his breach of faith.

The ambivalence between fear and hope in U.S.
policy has persisted into the present. We have fearfully
retreated from a strong policy because of the belief
that the Arab states might retaliate against America's
economic and strategic interests and that the Soviet
Union might gain prestige and power in a polarized
Near East. On the other hand, we have wishfully reached
forward into collaboration with the Soviet Union, mis-
judging the Russians and miscalculating their objectives.
We have allowed ourselves to be misled by the Russians
just as Mr. Chamberlain was misled by the Nazis—31
years ago today.

III. The Role of the United Nations

After the first Arab-Israeli war, Dr. Ralph Bunche,
the UN mediator, brought the parties together at
Rhodes, where they negotiated both directly and indirectly. Armistice agreements were signed between
Israel and four Arab states. But the parties interpreted
them differently. The Israelis viewed them as stepping
stones to peace. But the Egyptians argued that the
armistice agreements permitted them to remain in a
state of belligerence against Israel and that Egypt was
therefore justified in closing the Suez Canal to Israeli

shipping. In a historic ruling on September 1, 1951, the United Nations upheld Israel's contention that Egypt could not deny Israel shipping transit in the Suez Canal. The United Nations thus rejected the Egyptian thesis that she could remain indefinitely in a state of war. This remains a central issue of the Arab-Israeli conflict.

The United Nations has been powerless to enforce its rule and to cope with Arab violations. When Israel tried to test the issue again, the Soviet veto protected Egypt from censure and Egypt remained free to prosecute her blockade, to persist in belligerence.

The Soviet veto has blocked effective action by the Security Council. The Arab states can control one-third of the votes in the General Assembly with a coalition of Moslem, Arab, Soviet bloc, and Afro-Asian countries. The United Nations cannot be an instrument for peace in the Near East. Its agencies have served to keep Arabs and Israelis apart rather than to bring them together. It has become a conduit for the dissemination of anti-Israel propaganda because its decisions overlook or apologize for Arab aggression and provocation and censure Israel for her responses.

There is a double standard of expectations. Israel is expected to turn the other cheek—to turn the other plane, to roll with the punches, to accept aggression and infiltration, attack and subversion without protest, without response. The Jewish state is singularly honored.

Our country could counter the Soviet Union at the United Nations. But we have never used the veto except in the case of Rhodesia. We have gone along with one-sided resolutions. And these resolutions write a deplorable anti-Israel legislative history. The United States has not gained from this procedure. Not at all. The radical Arabs have always credited the Soviet Union for their support and initiative, and the United States is regarded as an unwilling tool and prisoner of diplomatic and political circumstances.

The 1957 experience is a prime example. When the United States and the Soviet Union joined in 1957 after the Suez war to force Israel to withdraw from Sinai and from Sharm al Sheikh, President Eisenhower promised, on February 20, 1957, that the Suez Canal would remain open to all shipping. This proved to be an empty promise.

When we allowed the Soviet Union to dictate the 1957 settlement, we enhanced its influence, with disastrous results. Jordan was compelled to oust its British officers and accept Nasser influence. Lebanon suffered a bloody civil war, aided and abetted by Nasserite agents and propaganda. Iraq killed its pro-Western leadership in the savage 1958 revolt. The next year Egypt closed the Suez Canal to Israeli shipping. But the United States did not move to protest. "Leave it to Dag," [1] said the Department of State.

As one positive result of the 1956 war, the Straits of Tiran were opened to Israeli shipping. This was backed by the reassurances of 17 maritime powers at the General Assembly. And the UN Emergency Force

(UNEF) was placed at Sharm al Sheikh to ensure it.

The Convention on the Territorial Sea and Contiguous Zone, adopted by the UN Conference on the Law of the Sea on April 27, 1958, by a 62 to 1 vote, and effective from September 10, 1964, declared:

> There shall be no suspension of the innocent passage of foreign ships through straits which are used for international navigation between one part of the high seas and another part of the high seas or the territorial sea of a foreign state.

But in 1967, UNEF garrisons at Sharm al Sheikh and in Gaza were blown away by Nasser's irresponsibility. UNEF was forced to withdraw. Israel's lifeline to Africa and the Orient was severed, and Israel was besieged.

What became of all the solemn commitments? We all know what happened. Nothing happened. No one was willing to move. Israel was isolated. The six-day war was the inevitable outcome.

IV. The Record Since 1967

When the six-day war ended in 1967, many thought that there was a real chance for an Arab-Israeli peace. We believe that two measures were essential:

1. To promote peace, urge the parties to talk over their differences in direct negotiations;
2. To prevent war, keep the Israelis strong enough to deter the Arabs and the Russians from military action.

To its credit, our government rejected Soviet demands that we pressure Israel to withdraw to the 1967 lines. Instead, our government argued that the parties themselves must reach agreement on frontiers as part of a comprehensive peace agreement.

The resolution unanimously adopted by the UN Security Council in November 1967 meant different things to the differing parties. The Arab states and the Soviet Union have insisted that the resolution obligated Israel to withdraw completely and unconditionally to the former armistice lines. But, to the United States and to Israel, the language and the legislative history meant that the frontiers had to be agreed upon by the parties.

Both the Arab states and Israel insist that they accepted the resolution. But while some Arab governments give lip service to the resolution, Syria, Iraq, Algeria, and the terrorist organizations will have nothing to do with it. Their declared objective is the liquidation of the State of Israel as a Jewish state. Arab leaders have emphasized that they cannot commit the Arab terrorists and that these organizations have the right to reject the resolution because it does not satisfy their objectives.

Thus, President Nasser told the Palestine National Council on February 1, 1969:

> The UAR appreciates the resistance organizations' stand in rejecting the Nov. 22, 1967 Security Council resolution, which the UAR has accepted.

It is the Palestinian organizations' right to reject this resolution. This resolution may be adequate to eliminate the consequences of the June 1967 aggression but it is inadequate to fulfill the Palestinian destiny.

Can this double interpretation be considered as a sincere acceptance?

The UN attempt to bring the parties together to implement the resolution failed. The Arabs blamed the Israelis, insisting that the resolution was self-executing. But the Israelis contended that it was up to the UN envoy, Gunnar V. Jarring of Sweden, to bring the parties together to reach agreement.

The Big Four Talks

Every new administration is the target of the Arab states and their many friends in this country who seek to change American policy. And so it was, when the Nixon administration took office in 1969 and we heard the question-begging propaganda for a "more even-handed policy." At that time, the administration, moved by fear of a great power confrontation and by hope for a détente, agreed to the French proposal for Big Power talks.

The Arab states were pleased. The talks relieved them of the necessity of negotiating an agreement with Israel. Professor Bernard Lewis, the distinguished British authority, wrote back in 1964 that the Arabs want an imposed settlement "in which, perhaps, Soviet arms would wield the knife while Western diplomacy administered the anesthetic." Moreover, the Arabs knew that the United States would be under pressure from the Russians and the French to accept their interpretation of the resolution.

The United States did in fact retreat on a number of major issues. This became evident in the proposals offered by Secretary Rogers in 1969 for Egypt and Jordan, proposals which critically undermined Israel's position in any future negotiations.

The Big Four talks provided a diplomatic cover for the Russians and Egyptians to make a giant leap forward. It is no coincidence that, as the talks began, Nasser was emboldened to renounce the UN cease-fire, which all the parties had accepted, and to open his war of attrition against Israel.

The Egyptian renunciation of the UN cease-fire should have brought worldwide condemnation and vigorous UN action to reinstate it. Instead, the violation was lightly condoned by the world community, as if Nasser, always immune and sacrosanct, were privileged to make war whenever and however he wanted to.

At the very least, our country should have provided Israel with all-out economic and military assistance. But we did not. Instead, we tried to set a righteous and noble example to the Russians by denying Israel's long-standing application for jet planes. This proved to be another dangerous miscalculation of Soviet objectives. Past experience with the Russians has shown that they will push aggressively into every corner where they encounter no resistance, that they will increase arms shipments precisely when we hold back.

As we held back, the Russians introduced their new missiles and their pilots. They shifted the balance of power in an attempt to gain mastery of the skies over the Suez.

What influenced our government's decision?

Some of our press like to exaggerate the strength of the so-called Israel lobby, with fulsome praise and pejorative innuendo. At the same time, they minimize the impact of the oil and diplomatic complex. This complex includes American diplomats in the field, who are on the receiving end of Arab threats and who relay them back to Washington, and it includes the prospectors, who dig for souls and oil. Members of this complex blame Israel as the scapegoat for all frustrations and setbacks. They hope to buy some space and time for themselves by rationing Israel's economy and defense. They think of short-range vested interests. They believe that we must placate the Arabs and that we will gain their affection only if we limit our support of Israel.

If the United States had made it clear in June 1967 that we were insistent on direct Arab-Israeli talks and that we would not become involved in any Great Power attempt to impose a settlement, and if we had extended military and economic assistance to Israel, we might have deterred the Soviet-Egyptian military buildup and we might have halted the Soviet Union's penetration of the region.

Later, Washington offered its new peace initiative: the reactivation of the Jarring mission and a 90-day truce period during which neither side would attempt to gain a new military advantage. This was partly inspired by Nasser's speech on May 1, in which he threatened to disrupt America's economic ties if we provided planes to Israel, but in which he indicated his willingness to accept a temporary cease-fire, if Israel would agree to withdrawal. Some Americans read between the bluster and perceived a very slim olive branch. At the same time the United States talked firmly and bluntly to the Russians, who had become arrogant and overbearing.

Seventy-nine senators, a remarkable coalition of Republicans and Democrats, of hawks and doves, joined in appeals to Secretary Rogers urging the administration to supply Phantom jets to Israel. More than a majority of the House took a similar view in a letter to President Nixon. These measures reassured the administration of congressional support for aid to Israel. More important, they served notice on the Soviet Union that the United States was not ready to abandon Israel.

Then came the strong declarations from President Nixon and White House aides intended to dissipate the dangerous impression that Israel's fate was not of vital interest to the United States. The White House warned that the situation in the Near East was more dangerous than the one in Vietnam, and made it clear that we would not permit the arms balance to be tipped against

Israel. The President went so far as to differentiate between the aggressive intentions of the Arabs and Israel's desire for peace. It was pointed out that the Soviet combat base in Egypt could transform the Mediterranean into a Soviet sea, obstructing the U.S. Sixth Fleet, putting land bases and oil supplies at the disposal of the Soviet Union and endangering moderate Arab regimes, NATO countries, and Iran.

In accepting the cease-fire proposal, both Israel and Egypt carefully spelled out their conflicting interpretations of the UN resolution of November 22, 1967. The Egyptians insist that Israel agree to withdraw from all territories. They have not budged from the Khartoum formula of 1967: "no recognition, no negotiations, no peace." The Israelis were finally willing to use the word "withdrawal," but they have made it clear that they mean withdrawal "to secure, recognized and agreed boundaries to be determined in the peace agreements."

The failure of the United States to note that reservation when it reported acceptance of the initiative to the United Nations alarmed Israel, and there was a brief diplomatic flurry between Washington and Jerusalem—which was swiftly superseded by the grave crisis over the missile buildup.

Throughout this period the United States has exerted strong pressure on Israel to be flexible and magnanimous. The Israelis have made important concessions, yielding on the question of time, place, level, and procedure. They agreed that the talks need not be direct. They also agreed to use the word "withdrawal," and to accept the U.S. assurance that there would be no buildup. They gambled on their security. They blundered. They would not do it again.

V. Why Israel Is a Vital Interest

I do not think it is necessary for me to try to justify Israel's right to exist. No state has such an impressive birth certificate.

Twice the international community has recorded its approval of the restoration of the Jewish people to their national homeland—once in the League of Nations and once in the United Nations. Mr. Eban has written that no state in the world expresses the concept of nation-hood more intensely than Israel. It is the only state in its area which bears the same name, speaks the same tongue, upholds the same faith, inhabits the same land as it did 3,000 years ago. The bitter history of the 1930s offered mournful testimony that there must be one place in the world where Jews may enter or live as of right and not on sufferance.

But Israel is more than a sanctuary for people. The Israeli government has demonstrated her capacity to govern and defend herself, to maintain the confidence and support of her people, to serve as trustee for their welfare and their rights, to revive the culture, ethos, and ethics of her finest prophetic era.

Many thoughtful Americans believe that Israel's sur-vival is consistent with America's interests—economic, strategic, and moral—and, despite the trend toward disengagement and isolationism growing out of the revulsion against our involvement in Indochina, there is ample evidence of American concern for Israel. Israel has proved to be a situation of strength, resisting the attempts of radical Arab states and the Soviet Union to dominate the Near East.

I believe that Israel and America are united by their common commitment to democracy and freedom. Israel is more than a democratic island resisting Communist pressure. Israel is an eloquent advocate of democracy and freedom, informing many people by example, instruction, and cooperation that independence for the state is not enough—that the individual must also be free and that men can advance to higher standards in a democratic and open society, that men will defend their institutions from aggression and subversion if they have a stake in their society as free, equal, and secure citizens.

We read in the press about the daily exchanges of fire across Israel's frontiers. What we do not read about —and what may some day prove of great significance in man's struggle for freedom—is the daily exchange of learning.

Israel's program of international cooperation today involves some 80 countries all over the world. Israel is a demonstration to the people of many lands that they do not need communism or fascism, that democracy is truly the best hope of mankind. Even our own country has something to learn from Israel's experience in education, in training, in combatting poverty and prejudice, in the integration of diversity. Each year more than 1,000 trainees arrive in Israel for courses in agriculture, labor, economics, science, and technology—some 12,000 in the last 11 years. At the same time, Israel annually sends out some 450 experts to help other peoples—3,000 to 64 countries in the last 11 years. The program continued despite the war, at a higher rate in 1969 than in 1968.

It is not strange that a people who cherished their land, who reclaimed it from centuries of neglect, erosion, and desolation, should be teaching and inspiring others to respect and preserve their patrimony, in mutual reclamation of land and people. Israel, the land which first proclaimed that men were equal before their maker, has become the most articulate exponent of democracy. It is a sad reflection that this democratic state has been besieged from the day of its rebirth and that the democratic powers have been so weak and grudging in their support.

It would be a mortal blow to America and to the humanitarian ideals for which she stands if Israel were compelled to succumb to the pressures of the Russian-Egyptian axis—if a democratic island were to be submerged by a tidal wave of brutal dictatorial force.

VI. What We Must Do

Just as long as the Arab states refuse to enter into negotiations for a genuine peace, we must take all pos-

sible measures to strengthen Israel's capacity and her
economy. The Arabs will never make peace with Israel
if they believe that they can destroy her while the
United States stands aside.

There should be no diminution or suspension of
American military assistance to Israel. And there should
be no misunderstanding either in Moscow or Cairo. If
we are indecisive, the Arab states and the Soviet Union
will feel free to press their war further.

We have been less than evenhanded. Over the years,
we have given $239 million in grant military assistance
to eight Arab states, and our economic aid and military
aid to Greece, Turkey, and Iran has been in the billions.
We have provided billions in aid to strengthen countries
which are on the Sino-Soviet periphery. Now for the
first time, Soviet military personnel have moved into
the Near East, along with huge quantities of armaments.
We have never given grant military aid to Israel, and
there has been an inexplicable reticence to provide arms
to Israel, while the Soviet Union has paced the arms
race in the Near East, pouring sophisticated weapons
into Egypt, Iraq, and Syria—much of it as a gift, much
for long-term low-interest loans.

Today Israel faces a much graver threat than ever
confronted most of the countries which have enjoyed
massive economic and military support from the United
States. The administration and Congress should consider
what can be done to help ease Israel's economic crisis.
Grant economic aid to Israel ended almost a decade ago.

Israel has had to pay high prices in life and resources to maintain her security and survival. If the Israeli citizen is defending the interests of the United States and the free world, we should not ask him to carry the entire burden alone.

Israel's defense expenditures have tripled since the six-day war. They were about 22 percent of Israel's gross national product in 1969, which is three times the proportionate burden borne by the United States, and they may rise to 30 percent in 1970. More than 90 percent of Israel's revenue comes from taxes. Furthermore, the Israelis have heavily mortgaged their future. *Israel's per capita foreign debt is the highest in the world!* It is obvious that Israel urgently needs large-scale economic assistance from friendly foreign governments to maintain economic stability.

The Soviet Union's military involvement in the Near East should be condemned by world opinion. We should mobilize other nations to join in the demand that Russian military personnel withdraw from Egypt. How can the Soviet Union pretend to be a peacemaker in the Big Four talks in the light of her military operations against Israel? We should not legitimize the Soviet presence on Israel's frontier. Israel must not suffer the fate of Czechoslovakia.

We should not condone Arab terrorism, nor should we reward, encourage, and recognize it by diplomatic gestures. We have just witnessed another shocking attack on innocent men and women, hijacked by the Arab terrorists in a desperate attempt to force the civilized world to yield to their demands. We must prosecute these criminals and insist that other nations act in concert with us.

We should isolate countries which harbor or subsidize the guerrilla groups. There is no glamor or heroism in a movement which "resists" Israel by hijacking and blowing up passenger planes, by murdering civilians in cafeterias and supermarkets, school buses and bus stations. The international community should impose sanctions against countries which provide sanctuary for terrorists who are involved in such action. We should not permit their planes to land at our airports, nor should our planes land at theirs. Criminals must be prosecuted. Violence cannot be justified by the argument that it serves a political objective, especially when that objective itself is an assault on the rights of others.

Above all, we should insist on a real peace. Arabs and Israelis must negotiate treaties. We cannot be satisfied with halfway measures which fall short of a real peace. We should reconsider our involvement in procedures like the Big Four talks which enable the Soviet Union to try to dictate the terms of a settlement and to entrench itself as the dominant power in the region.

The call for direct negotiations is not merely a bargaining tactic. Israel learned in 1949, during the successful Rhodes armistice talks, that agreements could be reached when she met directly with the Arab states. A principle is involved. The Israelis believe that if the

Arab states are not ready to meet and to negotiate the issues directly with them, they are not really ready to live in understanding and peace.

What the Israelis are looking for is more than uneasy coexistence. What they want is a full peace of sincere reconciliation which will end incitement to hate and which will open frontiers to an exchange of goods and goodwill—a cooperative effort toward security and a higher standard of living for all the people of the area.

Withdrawal

We should resist Arab pressures which call for Israel's total withdrawal from territories occupied in the six-day war. There is nothing sacred about the 1967 frontiers and there is nothing rational about the demand that Israel withdraw to them. Israel did not start the war of 1967 and those who began the war and lost it cannot claim to reinstate the vantage points from which they initiated their aggression and from which they may resume it.

I am well aware of the resolution which declares that territories should not be gained by conquest. But if that rule is to be applied to Israel, it must also apply to Jordan and to Egypt, for Jordan seized the West Bank and eastern Jerusalem in 1948 and Egypt seized Gaza. The United Nations never thought it necessary or expedient to demand their withdrawal from the territories they occupied. It was Nasser, not Israel, who massed huge forces in Gaza and Sinai in 1967. It was

Jordan which fired the first shots in Jerusalem. It was Syria which fired shots and dispatched terrorists from the Golan heights, and that irresponsible regime should not be permitted to use the Golan heights to shoot Israeli settlers and fishermen or to divert Israel's water sources.

If Israel is to withdraw, it must be to defensible frontiers, as Mr. Nixon has said. Her neighbors must obligate themselves to refrain from renewed aggression and there must be solemn undertakings to bar the use of their territories against her by military or paramilitary forces.

Why must Israel hold the Suez until there is a peace settlement? Because Israel's frontiers are now much shorter and more defensible than they were in 1967. Israel now, for the first time, has defense in depth. Her front lines are far removed from her populated cities.

Today there are more Arab soldiers on Israel's frontiers than in 1967, but the Israelis have not had to mobilize as they did in 1967, paralyzing their economy, for they not only have distance from the Suez Canal front but they also have the depth of the Canal to bar the advance of Egyptian forces.

Jerusalem

It has been said that Jerusalem is the most difficult problem. But I am convinced that an agreement can be reached to assure access to all the Holy Places for

all faiths because that has been assured throughout
Israel's administration since June 1967.

That was not the case when Jerusalem was divided
and when Hussein, in defiance of his obligation under
the armistice agreement, barred Jews from the Old City.
It was Hussein who permitted the desecration of Jewish
shrines and cemeteries. It was Hussein who kept the
Old City of Jerusalem and the West Bank *Judenrein*
for the first time in all history. He deserves no praise
from the international community.

The Refugees

The refugee problem must be faced by the Arab
states. It cannot be solved by Israel or at Israel's expense.

Those who espouse the Arab cause against Israel argue
that the refugee issue is the root cause of the conflict.
In truth, the refugee issue was the result of the conflict.
The cause was the refusal of the Arab states to accept
the international judgment that the Jewish people had a
right to restore their national life in their historic
homeland.

The Palestine Arabs were the victims of an injustice
perpetrated by the Arab states. They were offered their
own Arab state by the United Nations in 1947. But
that state was denied life by Transjordan, Egypt, Syria,
Iraq, and Lebanon, when they invaded Palestine to seize
it and divide it among themselves.

Long ago, the Arab refugees should have been welcomed and resettled in the Arab lands which have room

for them. But work projects which might have integrated them were opposed by the Arab states. Instead of accepting resettlement, the refugees were encouraged to insist on repatriation in a ritualistic repetition of an isolated clause (paragraph 11) in UN resolution 191 adopted in 1948. Those who cite that paragraph out of context, emphasizing the Arab shibboleth of repatriation, overlook the reality that the United Nations clearly intended that any such repatriation should be effected within the context of a peace settlement.

In the meantime, some 600,000 Jews have come to Israel out of Arab and other Moslem countries and there has been a de facto population exchange.

From the very beginning, the wisdom of resettlement and a population exchange was recognized by farsighted men. The British Labor Party in December 1944 adopted a resolution which even called for transfer of populations.

Here we halted half-way, irresolutely, between conflicting policies. But there is surely neither hope nor meaning in a Jewish National Home unless we are prepared to let the Jews, if they wish, enter this tiny land in such numbers as to become a majority. There was a strong case for this before the war, and there is an irresistible case for it now, after the unspeakable atrocities of the cold-blooded calculated German-Nazi plan to kill all the Jews of Europe. There is a strong case here, based on human grounds, for promoting stable settlement on the one hand and for the transfer of population on the other hand. Let the Arabs be encouraged to move out as the Jews move in. Let them be compensated handsomely for their land, and their settlement elsewhere be carefully organized and generously financed. The Arabs have many wide territories of their own; they should not seek to exclude the Jews from this small area of Palestine, which is less than the size of Wales. Indeed, we should re-examine the possibility of extending the present boundaries of Palestine by agreement with Egypt, Syria or Transjordan. Moreover, we should seek to win the full sympathy and support of both the American and Russian Governments for the execution of this Palestine policy.

Later, in 1949, the British recognized that resettlement was the major solution. Lord Henderson, speaking in the House of Lords, declared:

Until there is a peace settlement between the Jews and the Arabs, it will not be known what proportion of the Arab refugees can be repatriated. . . . But of greater effect will be a program of long-term constructive plans by which absorption and resettlement on a large scale can be carried out for those who cannot return to their old homes. . . . The sort of schemes I have in mind are a project for increased cultivation in the rain-fed Jezira area of Northern Eastern Syria; the irrigation of the Jordan Valley; and the irrigation of about two million acres in the Euphrates Valley in Iraq. . . . It is only by such projects that this urgent problem of the Palestinian refugees can be tackled with any success.

In our own country, both the Committee on Foreign Relations of the Senate and the Committee on Foreign Affairs of the House of Representatives have stressed the concept of resettlement.

It is totally unrealistic today to ask Israel to accept repatriation. Those who want to make Israel smaller and more difficult to defend also propose to legitimize her infiltration and penetration by those who have been killing her people in a senseless and stupid guerrilla war. How many of the heroes and hero-worshippers of the recent hijackings would be allowed to come back to renew their glorious war on school buses, passenger planes, and universities?

We are told that the Arab refugees were the victims of an injustice and that they are entitled to return to Palestine. But Palestine, it must be emphasized, was never an independent self-governing Arab country. It was part of an Arab empire which dominated the Middle East for just 434 years, almost a full 900 years ago. For much of its history Palestine was a desolate and neglected land of rocky eroded hillsides and mosquito-infested malarial swamps.

The Jews, who did have self-government or a measure of autonomy in Palestine for some 2,000 years—until they were subjugated by the Romans—always prayed for return. There were always some Jews in the country. And when the Jews came to rebuild Palestine more than a century ago, much of the land was owned by a few rich Arab absentee landowners, while the Arab peasants and Bedouins who lived in the country actually regarded themselves as Syrians, not Palestinians. Palestine was then known to the Arabs and to the world as southern Syria.

Prior to the Zionist reclamation, which began a full century ago, Palestine was a country of Arab emigration. But Arabs were attracted to Palestine by the Zionist development and many of the so-called Palestine Arabs are the sons and daughters of Arabs who came into Palestine from Lebanon, Syria, Iraq, and Egypt. If the Arabs had not made war against the Jewish state, many of them would still be there. Many are still in Israel. There are far more Arabs in tiny Israel than there are Jews in all the Arab states.

Many of the Palestinian Arabs are now in Jordan, which was part of Palestine until 1922, when Mr. Winston Churchill carved Transjordan away.

The Palestinian Arabs may be able to restore Jordan's original name—Palestine—and negotiate with Israel for territorial changes, for peace and secure borders. Instead of that, the program of the Palestinian terrorists calls for the seizure of Israel and the establishment of what is euphemistically described as "a secular state of Palestine" in which Arabs and Jews might live in blissful equality. However, the Jewish state would disappear under their program. Jews who came after 1917 would not be regarded as Palestinians. They would have to leave. In other words, Israel would cease to exist.

The irony of this preposterous Palestinian declaration is that no such egalitarian state exists anywhere in the Near East today—except Israel. Arab nationalism is intolerant of all minorities—the Copts in Egypt, the Kurds in Iraq, the Berbers in North Africa, the Blacks in Sudan. The notion that Jews would have equality in an Arab state is belied by centuries of discrimination and humiliation meted out to the stiff-necked Jews who refused to accept Mohammed's teachings.

Finally, it must be emphasized that the Arabs won their independence in vast areas. There are now 18 Arab countries, as a 1968 State Department document shows. They occupy an area of 4,600,000 square miles, more than $1\frac{1}{2}$ times the size of the continental United States. They are rich in oil, water, and arable land. And they have room. In equity, they who demand self-determination for themselves must be willing to extend self-determination to others.

Those who speak glibly of the elimination of the Jewish state and its replacement by another Arab state must ask themselves: Will civilization gain more by the creation of a 19th Arab state than it will lose by the elimination of the one Jewish state where the Jewish people are reviving their ancient prophetic and cultural heritage?

The sad fact is that the Palestinian al Fatah movement preaches hatred for the Israelis, not cooperation. They have made cooperation much more difficult by their incitement to kill Jews and to destroy their state. They have not succeeded in mobilizing Palestinian Arabs to revolt. But they have intimidated them from entering into a useful dialogue with the Israelis.

There are all kinds of nationalism, some benign and some baneful. Those who would recognize the Palestinians as a national entity should consider their objectives as they themselves have proclaimed them. Yasser Arafat, spokesman for al Fatah, said on May 5, 1969: "The main objective of al Fatah is to liquidate completely the political, economic and social existence of the Zionist base." And, speaking in Morocco on August 19, 1969, he stressed the point: "The objective of our war at this stage is to do away with the social, economic and political fortress of Israel in a long and protracted war which must of necessity end in success." Similarly, Dr. George Habash, leader of the Popular Front for the Liberation of Palestine, interviewed by Orlana Fallaci in *Life* magazine, June 1970, asserted: "We don't want peace, we will never agree to any peaceful compromise."

VII. Conclusion

In the Near East today we are witnessing a grim spectacle. Twenty-five years have passed since World War II witnessed the extermination of some six million Jews, the degradation of the survivors of that holocaust, and the desolation of the Jewish people around the world. At that time, the civilized international community reacted vigorously and, like the League of Nations after World War I, the United Nations reaffirmed the right of the Jewish people to establish its homeland in Palestine, with which it has been linked for thousands of years of recorded history.

But it is shocking to point out that the people of Israel, those who survived Nazi Germany, have lived to be shot at by the guns of every one of the five Big Powers.

There was a squalid war with the British. The French have armed the Lebanese, the Syrians, and now the Libyans. The Americans have armed the Iraqis, the Jordanians, the Saudis, and five other Arab states. The Communist Chinese have sent weapons to the terrorists. And the Russians have turned the military balance against the Israelis. Their military personnel have shot at Israel's pilots, while their Katyusha rockets have murdered Israel's civilians. Yet, never once during this long siege, has any one great nation been willing to allow Israel the gift of a single weapon.

Today, surrounded by hostile Arab states and Arab terrorists, the people of Israel are brutally threatened by the Soviet Union itself. It is a grim and terrifying spectacle which should shame the leaders of our civilized world who lack the courage and the morality to summon Israel's enemies to meet with her at the peace table.

The situation may get worse before it gets better. Yet we must not allow ourselves to be pessimistic about the long-range prospects of peace in the Near East. It may take a long time before the Arab states become reconciled to Israel's existence, and perhaps new Arab leadership may be needed. But I like to think that eventually the people of the Arab world will understand that they can live at peace with Israel and that they stand to gain more by reconciliation and peace than by hatred and war.

Both Arabs and Israelis struggled and won independence from foreign domination. But the people of Israel have gained something more than independence for the state. In Israel the people achieved freedom and equality for the individual, democratic institutions to enable them to find self-expression, social security to ensure them a stake in their country. This has not been the case in the Arab world where any experimentation with democracy has been short-lived and where people are ruled by military dictatorship or by feudal and dynastic regimes.

I am not suggesting that the way to peace is for us to promote new coups to overthrow the military dictators and thus to establish democratic societies. I leave that to the CIA.

I do submit that it is America's task to stand firmly with those who resist totalitarian aggression and who cherish freedom for the individual and democracy for their communities. If and when the ballot box replaces rule by rifle in the Arab Near East, perhaps we may hope for a change in the Arab attitude.

Meanwhile, if our government can make it clear to the Arabs, and to the Russians, that we are enlisted with Israel in the struggle for a genuine peace—and that we are enlisted for the duration and will not waver—the time may come when wiser men will come to power in the Arab lands to lead their people away from destruction and war to genuine cooperation and peace with all their neighbors.

SECOND LECTURE

ELMER BERGER

I. "Just Peace"—or Just Any Peace

Searching for a way to begin an examination of the subject of this seminar, I was helped by the Shakespearean passage used to introduce the first lecture in the American Enterprise Institute's earlier rational debate on the communications media of America.[1]

> Yet the first bringer of unwelcome news
> Hath but a losing office, and his tongue
> Sounds ever after as a sullen bell,
> Remember'd knolling a departed friend.

There is probably no area in American public affairs where it is easier to bring "unwelcome" (read "generally unreported") news, or to lose an office or sound "sullen" than the area assigned for discussion here.

One way to sound "as a sullen bell" and perhaps to invite the fate of a "departed friend" is to inquire, who specifically is prepared to take the title of this debate literally? The debate question suggests there would be a difference between a "just peace" and just any peace. I intend the emphasis on a possible difference to be more than just reaching for a *bon mot*. We have had "peaces" in Palestine before. The inventory could begin at the very beginning with the negotiations around the World War I era. There is the famous letter of the first Faisal to Frankfurter—a document which many believe has a dubious ancestry. There is the famous Weizmann-Faisal agreement from which, at least in the form most promoted to the Western world, a key paragraph was for a very long time (to use a polite term) neglected.[2] Both of these "peace" formulas contained stipulations in support of the Arabs. If respected, or enforced, they would have limited Zionist penetration of a demographically basic Arab territory; and so, hopefully, they might have forestalled, half a century ago, the impasse at which the world now stands in the Middle East.

Continuing the role of "bringer of unwelcome news," I find this is as good a place as any to refer to Arab contributions to the deterioration of the situation. For the most part, the circulation, promotion, and interpretation of these agreements were left to the Zionists and to the acquiescence of their sponsors among the Great Powers. One Arab-American scholar has commented about these and other agreements of those earlier years that:

> The Arabs themselves shared the responsibility for the suppression of these important documents by their failure to publish them in English and other major languages in order to explain and justify their own cause more effectively in the international propaganda campaign that was to develop over Palestine.[3]

The imbalance of information continues, although since June of 1967 there has been a gradual improvement, both of Arab effort and of receptivity on the part of the communications media of the Western world.

Probably because Arab reservations stated in these earliest agreements were swept aside, there were Arab rebellions in Palestine, of one magnitude or another, in 1920, 1921, 1929, 1933, 1936, and 1937-39. In one way or another, each was suppressed or "negotiated" to apparent pacification. But none of the "solutions" endured because for the most part they all either aimed at "just another peace" or, if there was the suggestion of coming to grips with the basic equities and political moralities, such a proposal was overturned by what might politely be called "nondiplomatic diplomacies" exercised against governments in either London or Washington. Both recently unclassified American[4] and British documents and the post facto judgments of responsible scholars offer ample documentary proof of this practice. One scholar has put it this way with respect to the years when the ultimate decisions were made in London:

> . . . [A] setback to Zionism incurred by the report of a commission which was sent to see for itself the cause of the troubles of Palestine was reversed by the activity of Zionist diplomacy in London. Through propaganda, political pressure, and the use of recruits of Zionism in high places, a govern-

ment policy decision based on the findings of its own commission was reversed.[5]

Secretary Forrestal, President Truman, Sherman Adams, Robert Murphy, to name a few, have all belatedly left carbon copies of just about the same plaint in the context of American policymaking.

II. The Inevitable Wars

This early history made the fighting of 1948-49 inevitable. During the previous three decades the Zionists had never imposed upon themselves any fundamental limitations to their historical goal of political domination of Palestine. Only on the rarest occasions did they accept a tactical defeat and this only *after* their "diplomacies" in London and/or Washington had yielded less than what they regarded to be satisfactory results. On the other side the Arabs never reconciled themselves to the increasingly threatening dimensions and exclusivist policies of the "national home." Whether because of their character or because they could not see their way clear to tactical accommodations without surrendering principles, their opposition was constant and unyielding. And without Arab protagonists in London or Washington, the major powers—to describe their actions charitably—allowed the situation to erode.

It is difficult to allocate blame among these several parties. A contemporary generation of Arabs has found the courage of self-criticism, identifying Arab lack of "know-how" in propaganda and general inefficiency as major contributing factors. The Great Powers for the most part engage in the usual incantations of self-righteousness. But the Zionists were, after all, the "newcomers" to the area—despite their pretensions to "historical connexion." They came as of "right"—according to the legal instruments relevant to the problem. But it was probably unnecessary for them to flaunt their "rights" and to flout the rights of those already there.

Ironically, it is in the bitter disillusion following the "glorious victory" of the 1967 war that some of the most dedicated Zionists are now admitting their early mistakes. Dr. Nahum Goldmann is an example. Former president of the World Zionist Organization and one of the architects of the State of Israel, his admission of guilt in 1969-70 came near to causing a government crisis in Israel when he said:

> . . . [H]owever legitimate its claims, the Zionist movement should never have lost sight of the fact that it represented an exception to the universally valid rule that a territory belongs to the majority of the population that lives there. In other words, from the ideological and ethical point of view as well as from the point of view of practical politics, Zionism should have tried from the first to reach an understanding with the Arab world.[6]

The diplomacies employed in the 1948-49 period are another effort at settlement which was allowed to dissipate by the same combination of Zionist aggressiveness, Arab incompetence, and Great Power acquiescence

or deliberate ambiguity. On December 11, 1948, the
General Assembly of the United Nations adopted Resolution 194. The resolution is best known for its paragraph 11, calling for "the refugees" to be permitted a
free choice between repatriation and compensation for
those who might elect not to return. But, in fact, the
thrust and implications of the resolution made it a kind
of mini-blueprint of the partition proposal of the
previous year and represented a new effort to make
that proposal operative through diplomatic agreement.
"Refugees" and the status of Jerusalem—to "be placed
under effective United Nations control"—were given
particular emphasis. But a "Conciliation Commission"
was established with instructions "to assist the Governments and authorities concerned to achieve a final
settlement of all questions outstanding between them."

Israel was not a member of the United Nations and
so could not vote. The Arab states opposed the resolution. Nevertheless, representatives of Egypt, Jordan,
Lebanon, and Syria were persuaded to meet in Lausanne,
Switzerland, in April of 1949. And there, together with
Israeli representatives, two identical but separate protocols were signed on May 12 by both Arabs and
Israelis. Maps were attached delineating the 1947 partition proposal's "boundaries." The signatories agreed
that this map should be the "starting point and frame-
work for the discussion of territorial questions." [7]

In the history of diplomacy over the Palestine question, these documents are known as the Lausanne Proto-

col. Together with the December 11, 1948 General
Assembly resolution, it practically revived the partition
proposal, taking into account the changed conditions
in Jerusalem and the "refugee" problem resulting from
the 1948 war.

On May 11, 1949, Israel was admitted as a member
state in the United Nations. The preamble to the admitting resolution stipulated, in explicit language, that the
General Assembly took "note" of the December 11,
1948 resolution and of Israel's declaration "in respect
of the implementation" of the resolution.[8] The General
Assembly understood, in other words, that Israel would
abide by previous UN formulas which, among other
things, recommended boundaries, the internationalization of Jerusalem, and provided the Palestinian refugees
with free choice between repatriation and compensation.

It is the diplomacy of this 1948-49 period which
has invested the 1947 partition recommendation with
greater sanctity in international law than any other
formulation of the Palestine problem. The Lausanne
Protocol is the only diplomatic agreement since 1948
to which both Israel and the Arab states most directly
involved have been signatories.

But once admitted to the United Nations, Israel
insisted that implementation of the previous formula-
tions, stipulated as conditions for her membership, must
await a final peace settlement. The Arabs, on the other
hand, insisted that implementation of the already legis-

lated resolutions must precede any final agreement and signing of a formal peace.

These themes still resound in the ears of the world, only at higher sound levels since June 1967. Israel claims to want only security. The two major Arab belligerents agree to the November 22, 1967 Security Council Resolution 242 which is, again, little more than a recapitulation of the outstanding issues, once more updated to take into account the consequences of the 1967 war. Once again—as in 1949—Israel is insisting, however, upon a formal peace before implementing, even in part, the fundamental principles inscribed in that document. And, again, "the Arabs" are insisting upon implementation of the principles as an earnest of justice before admitting even the hope of a peace. In 1949, the Arabs compromised their earlier position and agreed to partition provided Israel would withdraw to the boundaries suggested in the partition plan. Israel agreed but then welched with respect to the questions of boundaries and refugees. She moved her capital to Jerusalem in full defiance of the international call for internationalization.

Some justify Israeli defiance of the conditions for her admission to the United Nations on the grounds that "the Arabs" also failed to respect previous UN resolutions. Without wholly exonerating "the Arabs," it should be noted that their opposition came largely from Abdullah's Jordan. The Hashemite monarch saw a chance to realize, in part, an old dynastic aspiration to govern a "Greater Syria." With this motivation he annexed the West Bank areas of Palestine, including what was to become known as Jordanian Jerusalem. But it must also be observed that in March 1950 the Arab League denounced "Transjordan's efforts to annex part of Palestine and threatened her with expulsion." [9] That this action was motivated more by intra-Arab politics than by any affection for Israel does not negate the action itself. In its troubled history, Israel has known how to use internal Arab quarrels when it was to her advantage, and how to ignore these quarrels when it was also to her advantage.

Whatever the disparities in the accounts—and whatever details had still to be clarified and resolved—this spate of diplomacy in late 1948 and extending through much of 1949, represented the brightest hope for peace in the Palestine problem that the world had seen in the then 40-year-old conflict. Even taking into account Abdullah's recalcitrance, it is difficult to avoid the judgment that the major contributor to the failure was a State of Israel still unsatisfied with the partition boundaries, still hankering for control of Jerusalem, and still bent upon maintaining—by forceful opposition to repatriation of the Palestinians—the Zionist character of its society.

I am aware that in the inevitable and now familiar polemics in this problem, anyone who indulges in such a sojourn into history is tabbed with the epithets of "unrealistic," "pro-Arab," "romanticist," and even "anti-Semite." These are matched in kind, if not in quantity, by some from the other side who regard *any* bow in the direction of the facts of life—even if they are facts established by force—as puppets of the "imperialists," the "colonialists," and other targets of the Third World dogmatics. It is regrettable that so many people of integrity and moral courage in most matters have been "turned off" by this name-calling procedure.

If there is to be a "just" peace in the Middle East, in which the United States is to have anything constructive and worthy of its national character to contribute, many more Americans are going to have to acquire some knowledge of the facts and determine where the greater measure of justice is to be found. Then, having made this determination, they are going to have to rise above the practice of arguing this problem with more adjectives of sentiment than nouns or facts of history.

The collapse of the 1948-49 diplomacies made the 1956-57 war inevitable; and the failures, at the end of the Suez crisis, to follow through the disengagement processes with any genuine affirmations for an enduring peace made the 1967 war an equal certainty. It is now platitudinous to add that if the "initiatives" under way at this writing are also dissipated in name-calling, in fencing with symptoms rather than grappling with causes, and if basic, moral judgments are avoided, the next round is one of the few certainties in the generally amorphous world of international relations. With superpower polarization it is not necessary to elaborate upon the increased dangerous potential of such an eventuality.

III. What is "Just"?

The most important and contentious word in the title assigned to this seminar is, of course, "how"—*how* to achieve a just peace. Again, at the risk of sounding like Shakespeare's "sullen bell," I suggest the necessity of determining first *what* is a "just peace." Before we know what it is we cannot determine how to help realize it. And it is impossible to define what a "just peace" is without knowledge of the history which embraces whatever injustices exist. No court of justice limits its evidence to the time period beginning the day of a trial. Even the language of politicians describing their efforts as "evenhanded" is meaningless unless those words are related to some particular and recorded stage in the steadily downward spiral of this problem. For over 50 years, Zionist expansion of its ambiguous "writ" in the Balfour Declaration has given Zionism/Israel a constantly inflated idea of what should be its portion of an "evenhanded" division of the disputed issues. And, conversely, what might have been an "evenhanded" judgment for the Arabs in 1949 involved less of a loss than an "evenhanded" dispensation based upon the pragmatic geopolitical facts of 1970. Arab stubbornness and inflexibility have, without doubt, contributed mightily to the constant Zionist/Israeli escalation of force. This ingredient of international relations has been to the constant advantage of the Israelis and, accordingly, it can be said—by the pragmatists—that the Arabs have been their own worst enemies. But that judgment, all too frequently inserted as a consideration in the search for a "just peace," is irrelevant. One of Israel's most mature and distinguished academics, Jacob Talmon, put it bluntly to his own countrymen:

> Israel may be able to win and win and go on winning till its last breath, win itself to death, thereby demonstrating the truth of Hegel's aphorism about the "impotence of victory." [10]

For if a "just peace" is intended as an alternative to the prospect of more efforts to resolve the Palestine problem by more war, then historical evidence in the case of Zionism/Israel vs. "the Arabs" can be no exception. The second element, therefore, in the "how" of a just peace is a final disenchantment of the peacemakers with the idea of some great leap into a new future, deliciously iced with some frosting decorated to read "Let us forget all the nasty, unpleasant facts of the past and, beginning now, deal the cards, face up, from a fresh new deck." "Evenhandedness" will work only if it is determined first who suffered most and most egregiously and for what reasons, at whatever point the power centers of the world began to mark the cards.

It is not difficult to pinpoint that moment in history. Arthur James Balfour illuminated it in a long memorandum to his Cabinet in 1919. Challenged to rationalize the Balfour Declaration and the Palestine Mandate with Article 22 of the Covenant of the League of Nations, he wrote:

> Whatever be the future of Palestine it is not now an "independent nation," nor is it yet on the way to become one. Whatever deference should be paid to the views of those who live there, the Powers in their selection of a mandatory do not propose, as I understand the matter, to consult them. In short, so far as Palestine is concerned, the Powers have made no statement of fact which is not admittedly wrong, and no declaration of policy which, at least in the letter, they have not always intended to violate.[11]

Unfortunately, like most admissions of basic injustice to the Arabs, this one came two years after the fact. Even then, for more than 30 years it was a classified document to which only the British Cabinet was privy. This is not to say that others in the power structure of the world of that time were unaware of the discrepancy. In the United States the report of the King-Crane commission must have confirmed Woodrow Wilson's growing doubts about the consistency of the Palestine Mandate, embracing the Balfour Declaration, with his own ideals of self-determination. But that report, too, gathered dust for three years, after its delivery to an ailing President. The co-authors of the document, at a loss to explain its decline into obscurity but sufficiently protocol-conscious to refuse to divulge their findings themselves, "wondered whether Zionist opposition had not been a factor." [12]

Meanwhile, by the end of 1922 most of the major powers had agreed to most of the international agreements putting the Zionist camel's nose under the edge of the Palestine tent. The stage was set, therefore, for the ensuing 50 years of mounting hostility.

During these years, the world has largely ignored the fact that the Balfour Declaration explicitly limited what the British government might at any time consider to be its "best endeavours to facilitate" the Zionist "national home" project.[13] The limitations were dictated by respect for the rights of the Palestinian Arabs and the rights of "Jews in any other country." [14] The language used to introduce both of these "safeguards" is "it being clearly understood." Professor W. T. Mallison, Jr., who has pioneered among contemporary scholars in probing the legal questions involved in the whole Palestine affair, points to the difference between this phrase, "it being clearly understood," on the one hand, and the language used to introduce the "national home" clause of the declaration, on the other hand. Only "the best endeavours" of the British government were committed "to facilitate" the Zionist aspirations. After examining the negotiating history, Dr. Mallison concludes:

> The common feature of [the] two safeguard clauses was that each was designed to protect *existing rights* in the event of conflict with the British Government's political promise made in the first [national home] clause. In contrast to the ambiguities of the first clause, the safeguard clauses

were stated in unequivocal terms.[15] (Emphasis supplied.)

If the "realists" and "pragmatists" of the time had studied the history of Zionism from the founding of the movement in 1897 to their own days, they would not have expected the Zionist apparatus voluntarily to impose upon itself restraints out of deference to the rights of either the Palestinian Arabs or "Jews in any other country." For that history reveals a cavalier attitude toward the rights and the human dignity of the Palestinian Arabs. It also makes clear beyond all doubt that the Zionist apparatus did not limit its demographic aspirations either to upgrading the status of Jews already in Palestine or to achieving equal opportunities for immigration of limited numbers of Jews to the country.[16] The nationality constituency for which the Zionists claimed the mantle of authority was something called "the Jewish people." The Zionist political campaign was designed to establish the "right" of "the Jewish people" in Palestine. It was not limited to establishing the "rights" of Jews who might voluntarily elect to make Palestine their home. There is all the difference in the world between the two objectives. The one presumed "the Jewish people"—all Jews—possessed a second set of national rights and obligations in and to a territory already inhabited by a majority of people who were not Jews. In addition to the inevitable aggression against the indigenous Palestinians, this Zionist policy constituted aggression against all Jewish nationals

of "any other country" who did not wish the status of
dual nationality predicated upon their Jewish identity.
The failure or willful refusal of the world's statesmen
to see the difference between this claim and some
formula assuring Jews equal opportunity in a potentially democratic Palestine is another way of describing
the germinal origins of the present conflict.

Both of these aggressions, over the years, produced a
responsive defense by the injured parties. One Arab
scholar, for example, has said:

> Long before "wars of national liberation" had
> become fashionable in Asia and Africa in the sec-
> ond half of the twentieth century, the Palestinian
> people was waging its own costly and persistent
> war of national liberation in the form of rebellions
> directed against both British rule and the Zionist
> program.[17]

That perspective on the Palestinian resistance may
surprise a number of policymakers and peace seekers.
But it will probably be as bland as a weather report
compared to the generally suppressed, or certainly
ignored, fact that there has been a consistent anti-
Zionist position among Jews for all these years. The
so-called "safeguard clauses" in the Balfour Declaration were probably largely a result of the influence of
these anti-Zionist Jews in England at the time, led by
Edwin Montagu.[18] It may surprise casual dabblers in
the Palestine problem even more to learn that some of
the most vigorous anti-Zionism was publicly and systematically expressed by some of the most observant

and orthodox Jews of the world, living in Palestine itself.

> With regard to the Zionists what shall I say and what am I to speak. . . . The chief of these ruffians in our Holy Land has uttered terrible words, full of denial of the Most High, promising that Dr. Herzl [19] will neither rest nor be silent until the foot of Israel ceases from the lands of Exile, and mocking at the saying of the sages that the day of the Gathering of the Exiles will be as great as the day on which heaven and earth were created. . . . And had I intended to describe to your honour the storm that was aroused among the masses of Arabs and Christians, I would have insufficient paper and been too weak to elaborate. . . . For us in the Holy Land it is a sure sign that Dr. Herzl comes not from the Lord but from "the side of pollution". . . .[20]

Those are not the words of Gamal Abdel Nasser, or even the Grand Mufti, but of a distinguished rabbi, Joseph Hayyim Sonnenfeld, written from Palestine to a colleague in Hungary in 1898.

In its contemporary form in the United States, adherents to this anti-Zionist tradition have frequently petitioned the U.S. government to enforce recognized constitutional and statutory restrictions upon the operations of the Zionist/Israeli nationality mechanism in the United States. On April 20, 1964, the then Assistant Secretary of State Phillips Talbot, following a long and complicated correspondence, did state, in a letter addressed to me, that the United States did not recognize Zionism's "Jewish people" nationality concept as a valid concept of international law. But as with so many anti-

Zionist policy decisions or decisions designed to safeguard Palestinian Arab rights, this one continues to
be honored more in the breach than in enforcement.

From the very beginnings of its status as the "public
body" it is designated to be in Article 4 of the mandate,
the World Zionist Organization has ignored the rights
and views of *all* anti-Zionists, whether Christian or
Moslem Arabs in Palestine or "Jews in any other country." What is less understandable and less defensible is
that both of the Great Powers which over these 50
years have served as principal patrons of the Zionist
establishment have not only indulged these illegalities,
they have also, directly or indirectly, subsidized them
with money and encouraged them by a steady stream
of either earnest or tongue-in-cheek endorsements.

So, the excursion into history suggests another "how"
in the difficult job of fashioning a just peace in the
Middle East. But first, again, the peacemakers must
decide what is just. If they wish to perpetuate a situation in which one party to the conflict is "the sovereign State of the Jewish people," [21] rejecting the
recognized rights of the Palestinians in the interest of
Jews in other countries who are presumed to possess a
functional dual nationality, there is very little hope for
peace. But if there is a relationship between justice and
law, then the Zionist apparatus should be brought to
the bar for violating the laws which are designed to
protect the integrity of most sovereign states in general,
as well as for violating the specific safeguard enactments

which were designed originally to protect the rights of
anti-Zionist Jews and of the Palestinian Arabs.

If anything I have said so far is "unwelcome news"
with the tone of a "sullen bell," this recommendation
will toll a tune of exquisite pain to the politicians.

In recent years, from Franklin Roosevelt's long suppressed agreement with Ibn Saud to consult the Arabs
fully before making any final determination about
Palestine,[22] through Harry Truman's post facto com-
miserations with his own *Memoirs* over Zionist pressures,
through Dean Acheson's confessions on the same era,
through John Kennedy's still mostly mysterious correspondence with Nasser, through the gyrations of
Eisenhower and Dulles over the Suez Canal crisis and
the Aswan Dam, through the still unexplained chem-
istry which backed Lyndon Johnson away from the
American guarantee for the territorial integrity of *all*
the Middle Eastern states, and through Richard Nixon's
assignment of Governor William Scranton to a back-
burner following his "evenhanded" recommendation at
the end of 1968, all American administrations—and
their coattail colleagues in Senate seats or the House of
Representatives, in governors' chairs or city councils—
have played fast and loose with both the facts of history
and with American interests.

IV. "Political Legitimacy"

Some months ago I was slightly encouraged to hope
for a new era—at least in the White House. Profiles of

important personalities in *Life* magazine are not one of my usual sources of documentary information about problems as difficult and complicated as that of Palestine. But in its September 5, 1969 edition, *Life* had a profile of Henry Kissinger. A good deal of a not overly long article was devoted to problems in and about Israel. The subject was raised in the context of a conversation between Kissinger and the Israeli general who had captured Jordanian Jerusalem in the 1967 war. The general was described as a friend of Kissinger and on a personal visit. Kissinger disagreed with him about how long Israel could continue to hold the territories occupied in June 1967 in order to bring the Arabs into negotiation and conclude a contractual peace. The Israeli saw virtually no time limit. Kissinger argued that eventually world opinion would force Israel to reconsider. Finally, the Israeli asked Kissinger what alternative he had to offer, and the principal foreign policy aide on the President's staff replied: "The question before Israel is whether it can trade some of its physical superiority for some political legitimacy." [23]

The so-called operative words in that meaningful sentence are very broad, indeed—perhaps deliberately so. But some analysis of these words may suggest some concluding "hows" of a just peace in the Middle East.

The first noteworthy observation is that Dr. Kissinger left the initiative to Israel. This, in itself, is a kind of heresy for which others—Senator William Fulbright and Senator Mark Hatfield as examples—have been put on the rack. But it is now clear that regardless of who offers the advice, left to its own devices, Israel will not take any such initiative. It has come where it is by its "superior physical force." That force is not alone military. Israel also enjoys superiority of economic and technological development. Since statehood, the Zionist presence in the Middle East has been prodigally helped to this advanced economic condition by the generosity of the United States. Responsible estimates run to the figure of $4 billion.[24]

But perhaps the most significant phrase in the broad statement is "political legitimacy." The most obvious implication of the exhortation to Israel to achieve this status is that it does not now enjoy it. It would have been a genuinely constructive exercise in politics, law, and semantics had Dr. Kissinger amplified what he meant by the phrase. Some known fact situations, however, make some clarification and refinement of Kissinger's broad language possible without implying these were the considerations in his own mind.

It may be futile to try to lay a persistent and moldy Zionist propaganda ghost before it frightens away even any timid application of fact and law, but it is perfectly clear that Kissinger does not deny the existence of the state. Nor is he advocating "driving it into the sea." We have had a surfeit of these Zionist-concocted false dilemmas. "Love it or leave it" attitudes are anything but helpful in such complicated problems and the Zionist/Israeli muckraking has—for too long and unchallenged—been permitted to "hang-up" the American people on such fabricated alternatives. There is some evidence that the generally uncritical use of Zionist/ Israeli handouts by the American communications media in 1967 has now been replaced with a slightly more sophisticated accounting of events and a somewhat more realistic estimate of responsible critics of Zionism/Israel as, after all, humans.

The second speculation about Kissinger's pitch for "political legitimacy" assumes he sees a relationship between such legitimacy and law; and it assumes that while he recognizes Israel as a de facto state, the state's persistent defiance of most international agreements which in any way could be interpreted as legitimatizing its existence and the enforcement of this defiance by "physical superiority," leaves the question of its "political legitimacy" open to question. In the context of this constant use of force in the absence of compliance with law, Gamal Abdel Nasser's observation that "the last word in our struggle will be force" [25] is understandable. It is not that "the Arabs" love to fight. It is rather because the world, indulging Israel's flouting of the law, appears to have left no other recourse. The only escape from that vicious circle, which has been growing tighter and tighter around the Middle East for 50 years, is to have a breakthrough of law. Perhaps it can be assumed, therefore, that someone of Kissinger's stature and knowledge means Israeli compliance with— or at least negotiation based upon—the principles and recognition of the historic, outstanding limitations upon the territorial and demographic aspects of the Zionist state. That is to say, "political legitimacy" involves Israeli recognition of the "inalienable right" of the "Palestinian people" [26] and borders somewhere around those suggested in the 1947 partition recommendation. It must also mean some form of international control of Jerusalem. Those were essentially the ingredients of the broad agreements signed in Lausanne in May of 1949. Only a fool would predict with any certainty that *anything* will substitute peace for war in this problem. But there is some reason to hope that once a commitment to law is made, areas of compromise between the parties could be found. Fundamental to that hope, in my opinion, is the prior Israeli acceptance of the principles involved in the law already written on these three basic issues of "refugees," borders, and Jerusalem.

Israel is reluctant to accept these inscribed international agreements as negotiating principles. They clearly adumbrate that for all these years Zionism/Israel's "rights" in the area have been questionable. Somewhere, Kissinger must have come to this realization. Otherwise it is difficult to explain his recommendation that Israel now try for "political legitimacy."

V. The Palestinians

Four or five years ago these three items might have completed the agenda for negotiations. They could have resulted, as the Lausanne agreement would have, in a "little Israel"—a small Zionist state with, to be sure, a precarious "Jewish" majority. But it is a classic pattern in these protracted and bitter quarrels that the longer they are allowed to endure the higher the price for settling them. Control, on both sides, slips from the hands of the moderates and is eagerly grasped by the purists and the hard-liners. Indulgence of Israel's policies of the past three years, of attempting to force peace based upon its military victory in 1967, has created a new formidable factor in the Palestine problem. The Palestinians—the resistance—now exercise an indeterminate but no longer ignorable influence. Whatever the results of present efforts at diplomacy, in this autumn of 1970, the Palestinian "revolution" will be a factor in the Middle East for a long time. It may regroup its force and reorder its priorities. But it will not go away. On the contrary, it can be cautiously speculated that if a peace should be achieved as a result of present efforts, "revolutionaries" in both Israel and the Arab world may join forces for altering the whole social, economic, and political character of the entire area. This is probably a discordant note to inject here, for to the extent this speculation may project the shape of things to come, it provides many interests with something less than undiluted motivation to find a formula for settlement. Perhaps the most effective single argument for struggling to find a formula for peace anyhow is that the perpetuation of the 50-year-old conditions for war will only quicken the "protest" everywhere and keep its attention riveted on destructive purposes. In a context of peace and with some diligent application of some of the enlightened self-interest policies the liberal forces in the world have learned, there may be a chance to channel the energies of this new breed in the area into constructive works.

In any event, to return to the more immediate business of the "hows" for a just peace, there are now voices on both sides of the cease-fire lines calling for a "de-Zionized" Israel. If it will not appear immodest, I believe I was the first ever to use the term and to argue for the application of its substantive meaning to the Palestine problem. My motivation, in the first place, derived from the historic Jewish anti-Zionist tradition which holds that the fundamental factor identifying a Jew is Judaism. And Judaism is a system of religious thought and belief. It is not—and it has not been for at least 2,000 years—a system of political-national rights and obligations. Deny it as they have—and often still do—Zionists regard every Jew as the possessor of a functional "Jewish people" nationality. In their "public relations," tailored to the integrated Jews of the free world, the Zionists camouflage the real character of their program. They appeal to "charity," to "culture," to "unity" on the positive side and they stimulate support by inspiring negative reactions against "the Arabs" and by labelling critics of Israel as "anti-Semitic." These appeals to vaguely felt sentiments, on the positive side, and to common "enemies" on the negative side, give an appearance of solidarity which is denied by the sociological facts.

These propaganda ploys, however, would not have sufficient adhesive power if the majority of free-world Jews really knew the facts of Zionism/Israel's political-legal claims. And one of the major contributing factors to the deception is the politicians who either do not know the truth themselves or are too mendacious to speak it, if they do know it.

The State of Israel has no constitution. In its place there exists a category of legislation called "basic" or "fundamental" laws. Israel's "Law of the Return" is one of these. It automatically confers Zionism's "Jewish people" nationality on every Jew. Israel's "Nationality Law" makes this "Jewish people" nationality *automatically* convertible to Israeli citizenship the moment any Jew enters the country, if he or she has not rejected the functional "Jewish people" nationality *prior* to entry. Despite the April 20, 1964 letter from Assistant Secretary of State Phillips Talbot rejecting "the Jewish people" as a concept of international law, specific rulings of one or another branch of our government have been less than precise.[27]

To the Arabs, this "Jewish people" functional nationality represents the legal basis for what in more general language is called "expansionist Zionism." This is stated more explicitly by the Palestinians than by others. In plain language, this "Jewish people" nationality is an open-ended, even if a unilateral, obligation on the part of the Zionist State of Israel to take in every Jew in the world. "Fundamental" Israeli legislation describes "Ingathering the Exiles" as the "central task" of the state. "The World Zionist Organization/Jewish Agency (Status) Law, 5713-1952" licenses that organization to mobilize "the Jewish people" in support of the state and to recruit immigrants to populate the state.[28] Introducing this legislation to the Knesset in 1952, the then prime minister, Mr. Ben-Gurion, candidly admitted the purpose:

> However unique is the State of Israel in the manner of its emergence and its task, it is obliged to operate like every other state, and *its capacity outside its borders is restricted*. It is the Zionist Organization, built upon the voluntary association and activity, *which is able to achieve what is beyond the power and competence of the State*, and that is the advantage of the Zionist Organization over the State.[29] (Emphasis supplied.)

The Zionist movement is doing precisely this in the United States and in other "affluent" nations. There are immigration recruiting centers in numerous American cities and their efforts are financed, largely, with American dollars raised as "humanitarian charity." [30] An authoritative report in July of 1970 indicated that "more than 1,200 people" would be going from America to settle in Israel in this one month.[31]

The Arabs see this organized, sustained, generously financed campaign to bring in more Jews, together with

Israel's policy of steadily pushing out the borders into Arab lands—and the permissiveness of the Western powers toward both prongs of this aggression—as a fundamental obstacle to any enduring peace.

The Zionist/Israeli establishment is not at all reticent about relating this immigration to its geopolitical and demographic aspirations. Most Americans, including most American Jews, are subjected to adrenalin-stirring pitches for "rescuing" Jews believed to be in peril of their lives. Not so the Zionist/Israeli pitchmen. Part of the problem is that their cool candor is expressed in places where the American public, and even most of our informed policymakers, rarely inquire for the facts. For example, in 1968—a little more than a year after the 1967 war and while Israel was striving to impress the world that all it wanted was "security"—the official *Reports* of the Twenty-Seventh Zionist Congress in Jerusalem was observing:

> The crucial question confronting us is how are we to populate with Jews the newly-liberated areas, at a time when Jews living in countries from which egress is possible are unwilling to come and settle here.[32]

The same official source advises that "in the 1966-67 fiscal year . . . 40% of the total immigration to Israel came from 'affluent countries' and in the first nine months of 1967-68 'passed the 40% mark.' "[33]

Now it is crucially important to make it emphatically clear that none of this is conspiratorial. These

combined actions of the Zionist organization and the
Israeli government are not the fancies of some fevered
brain in the Zionist/Israeli establishment, nor of some
lunatic fringe racist in the United States, reeling from
an encounter with the Protocols of the Elders of Zion.
All of this—and more than space permits here—is published in official documents of the Israeli government
and/or the World Zionist Organization. Much of it is
on file with the U.S. Departments of Justice and State.
Our daily newspapers rarely miss a day when there is
not at least one story illuminating one specific detail of
the on-going implementation of these policies. There is,
therefore, no valid reason for not raising these items
on any agenda for a truly "just" peace in the Middle
East.

What is lacking in the United States is the will on
the part of our responsible governmental authorities
not only to examine the evidence, but to draw the
proper conclusions and then to take appropriate action.
As one who, over a period of many years, has presented
much of this information in documented form to com-
petent authorities of our government, I make that
statement on the basis of first hand knowledge. Too
often the reply has been, "But you are reading the fine
print."

And so there is little reason to believe that, left to
its own devices, Israel will take the initiative to establish the "political legitimacy" which Kissinger seemed
to suggest would be in its own interest. With all apolo-

gies to the "pragmatists" of the National Security
Council, a 50-year-old pampered child is unlikely sud-
denly to refashion its life pattern, voluntarily slough
off its exploitation of overweening parents, and elect
to stand on its own merits in the hurly-burly of the
rough-and-tumble world. But there is another possible
approach. That is for the super-indulgent parents to
leave off "sparing the rod and spoiling the child." To do
this in the historic context of Zionist associations with
the U.S. government will invite the full energies of the
Zionist/Israeli establishment to make the shift look like
infanticide—or, if you prefer Mr. Abba Eban's coin-
age, "politicide." But if Mr. Kissinger reflects anything
of the thinking of the Nixon administration and if—
which would be hard to believe—his inference that
Israel's existence lacks "political legitimacy" was not a
slip of the tongue, then both the integrity of the American character and the specifics of American legislation
exist as ways to contribute to the process of legitimatizing. Zionism/Israel's "Jewish people" nationality is inconsistent with the Constitution of the United States.
We cannot force Israel to surrender it. But we can
refuse to permit its application to Americans and we
can deny the Zionist state the privilege of subsidizing
its "Jewish people" nationality apparatus with tax-
deductible American dollars. We cannot force the government of Israel to abrogate its 1952 Status law, which
licenses the Zionist movement to serve the State of
Israel inside the borders of other states where the Israeli

state itself cannot legitimately operate. But we can stringently apply the Foreign Agents Registration Act. What all the available evidence indicates "is in some aspects a part of the Government of Israel and in others a public-body agent of that Government which performs particular tasks for it" [34] would then be easily identified by the American people.

VI. "The Nerve of Failure"

Such actions by the U.S. government would at least legitimatize our own political and financial posture toward Israel. They would be in respect of our own value system and consistent with specific legislation.

I do not argue such actions would, of themselves, produce peace in the Middle East. But I believe they would help. And I am certain they would be long strides forward toward reestablishing respect and admiration for our country in that area where, 50 years ago, the majority people, faced with the inevitability of the mandate system, wanted the United States to assume the Mandate for Palestine. After half a century of British and then American indulgence, it is difficult to predict how far Israel might go on its own effort to force down the throats of its Arab neighbors the latest accomplishments of what has often been called its fait accompli diplomacy. As a practical matter, Israel's dependence upon the United States for both military hardware and funds to sustain its civilian population's standard of living [35]—while it continues to occupy ter-

ritory acquired by force—warrants the cautious guess
that the Zionist establishment in the Middle East could
not go very far, "going it alone."

This does not mean we must abandon this state,
however ill advised were our past policies which played
the major role in its establishment and in sustaining it.
Certainly we can distinguish between the excessive
permissiveness of this past support on the one hand, and
defensive support on the other, while a repentant Israel
is encouraged to normalize its sovereignty as an important element in any formula for living with its neighbors. This is the only hope that the legitimate citizens
of the territory it now occupies will experience as much
security as anyone knows in this agonized world.

Even if the exercise of such American persuasion
predicated upon fundamental American values and
important American law did not persuade Israel to
seek such normality, our own integrity could be restored.
We may no longer even aspire to play the role of world
policeman. But we are certainly powerful and prestigi-
ous enough to be captains of our own soul. And the
entire conceptual basis of Zionism and the state it has
built in the Middle East is inconsistent with everything
Americans have been taught to believe about themselves
and the purposes for which they should exert influence
in the world.

It could be said to Mr. Kissinger, therefore, that if
his advice to Israel to seek "political legitimacy" is really
serious, he is in a very strategic spot to begin the process

by legitimatizing the relations of our country—and particularly its citizens who are Jews—to the Middle Eastern state. Israel may take the cue, or not. But Mr. Kissinger—and the government of the United States —would enter any pleadings with cleaner hands than it now possesses.

This paper is deliberately addressed to the assigned question of a "just" peace in the Middle East. I have not examined the substance of a peace tailored in the American interests. I have hardly intimated any appreciation of the shifting geopolitical situation resulting from the dramatic shrinkage of our country's prestige in most of the nation states from Morocco to the Persian Gulf. If I have seemed to be partisan it is because the "original sin," [36] as one Israeli has put it, was committed by Zionism and supported by its patrons, who by superior force put the Zionist establishment into the Middle East against the will of the majority population of Palestine. Until that sin is at least confessed and put out into the open, there will be neither the psychological nor the moral climate in which any peace worthy of the name can be established. I have paid little deference to the habitual condescensions of American politicians to the Zionist machine and its never-demonstrated capability of delivering a "Jewish vote." There is very little doubt that we are where we are in the Middle East because this element in the "old politics" has played too decisive a role for far too long.

That I have not examined any of these phenomena here in depth should not be construed to mean I am unaware of them. We were not invited to devise a politically safe or a geopolitically invulnerable peace— or an America *uber alles* peace.

For good or bad, the United States made decisions years ago about this inflammable problem. Nations, like people, have to live with the consequences of their choice. But only decadent nations and extraordinarily puerile politicians insist upon compounding errors to the point of total destruction of self-interest and the abasement of revered values. In my judgment, the greater weight of our national interest, our respected national values and our geopolitical concerns coincide, in this problem, with a dedicated effort first to acknowledge the large measure of justice which history indicates is on the side of "the Arabs." When we have done that —and only then—can we construct national policies which may be a contribution to a "just peace." Whatever political naiveté may appear to motivate this recommendation is no greater than all the "realistic" maneuvering in which our statesmen have engaged for half a century. The proof of the pudding is in the eating of the bitter failures and the threatened American interests all of these realists have produced.

There may now be a kind of poetic justice in the frightening possibility that in what is loosely called "the Holy Land" American political leadership is faced with a choice between long evaded moral considerations and a potential Armageddon. For a long time our political leaders have had a free ride in that area of the world. While we eloquently declaimed our Jeffersonianism to the rest of humanity and allowed the Zionist/ Israeli propaganda machine to portray its Middle Eastern state as a small carbon copy of our own vast power and prestige, we were really hiding our heads in the sands to avoid the truth which really makes us all free.

I do not know that the recent initiatives will bring a "just" peace to the Middle East. There are those who doubt that in any foreseeable future any peace is possible. Precisely because the spectrum of possibilities stretching from a "just" peace to just any peace to no peace at all is so broad and because the issues are so old and encrusted with emotion and misunderstanding, any success will require more than the usual concentration and energy.

In this situation, as in most such situations, there are uncounted numbers of people who want peace. And in this situation, as in so many others, it is possible that governments are frozen into patterns which have been obstacles to peace in the past. In such situations, while not at all minimizing the importance of the amenities or the relationship between tactics, strategies, and objectives, bold and imaginative leadership may be the most important "how" of the way to a just peace. I believe the American people would support such leadership, if they are told what facts motivate it. The American government is capable of stating those facts—for they are all available—if it only will. What can defeat this new, so-called American initiative is what has hamstrung us in the past—a failure of political nerve.

Since I am not a politician, my advice for an antidote may be politically worthless. But I suggest it anyhow. To do so, I borrow the words of a distinguished American sociologist, David Riesman, who has recommended, as a formula for these troubled times and for such troubled problems, the possibility of testing the "nerve of failure." That is perhaps a modern academic's formulation of the essence of the great prophetic tradition of the Judeo-Christian heritage which we are fond of identifying as the very bedrock of our national existence.

What more fitting place to test "the nerve of failure" than to apply that tradition to the cradle lands from where, in the distant but still cherished past, this tradition came!

THIRD LECTURE

ALLEN POLLACK

In seeking to clarify the most important issues involved in the Middle East, at least three major conflicts in the area should be traced.

The first, and of course, the most familiar of these conflicts is the continued state of war between Israel and the Arab states. The conflict is bitter and genuine rights are involved on both sides. Interestingly enough, however, the outstanding points of this conflict, which is primarily a dispute over territory, could lend themselves fairly easily to compromise. The Security Council Resolution of November 22, 1967 contains the outline of the most feasible settlement. Unfortunately, such a solution is unlikely to come about, because these issues involving territory, the Arab refugees, the city of Jerusalem, or navigation rights through international waterways are but the surface reflections of the more basic forces which underlie the conflict.

The fundamental question is still whether the Arab states are ready to accept the existence of a viable Jewish State of Israel as an equal in their midst. So far it remains a fact that they are unwilling to face reality—they are unwilling, in spite of three humiliating defeats in 20 years, to give unqualified acceptance to the fact of the existence of the sovereign State of Israel. Their unwillingness reflects their deep-seated resentment of what Israel represents in their eyes. It also reflects their frustration and bitterness at their inability to solve the anguishing problems which beset their own societies, as these societies are being forced into a process of dramatic change and social transformation. These processes are more important to the future of Arab society than is any basic clash of nationalisms, such as that which the Arab-Israeli dispute also reflects. This helps explain the continued unwillingness of the Arab states to entertain any compromise in their fundamental opposition to the legitimacy of Israel's existence.

In recent years, the Arab-Israeli dispute has become more complicated with the emergence of Palestinian nationalism. There are now two components to the conflict, related though separate. In the straightforward dispute between Israel and the Arab states the outstanding issues still lend themselves to fairly easy resolution. However, the dispute between Israel and the Palestinians may be much more difficult to resolve if Palestinian nationalism develops only in an extremist form, as is the case at present—if, that is, no alternative force representing the true interests of the Palestinians emerges to the present guerrilla groups, who define their *minimal* demands as including the dissolution of the State of Israel as presently constituted. In spite of the depth of feeling involved, the Arab-Israeli dispute is actually less important in the Middle East context as a whole than the other conflicts with which it has become intertwined.

The second major conflict in the Middle East concerns the very reason why the area is both so prominent in the news and so menacing to world peace. The Middle East has become the newest and most volatile front, reheating the cold war between East and West. The world can tolerate, as it has in the past, festering wars between small nations. But it cannot survive direct clashes between the Great Powers. This is the war that must be defused, for it contains the threat of potential global destruction. Because of Great Power involvement, the Arab-Israeli dispute has remained unsolved. Because of Soviet actions in recent years, the stakes have been raised, and the issues now far transcend regional considerations.

The third major conflict in the Middle East is the incessant internecine warfare going on inside the Arab world itself. This state of affairs also serves to clarify the Arabs' continued intransigence on the issue of Israel. It is also one of the reasons why the Soviet Union has been able to penetrate into the area so swiftly and easily. These constant internal convulsions are the Middle East variation of the overall struggle for modernization in the underdeveloped world. They reflect the effort of an undoubtedly great people to make the basic social, political, economic, and even cultural changes necessary to transform their societies into modern nation states.

Within the context of struggle and change the rulers of the Arab world have used war with Israel as a means of maintaining themselves in power. To some, the State of Israel has become a convenient excuse for their inability to solve their own domestic problems. To others, it has become the focal point towards which they seek to divert those forces threatening revolutionary change. To all the Arab leaders, Israel has come to serve as a means of uniting a people otherwise deeply rent by splits and fissures. Hostility towards Israel also serves as a foil for their frustrations at their own inability to reach out of their own backwardness. Ironically, in the Middle East, Israel plays the same role that the Jews traditionally played in Eastern Europe. It serves as the scapegoat for the domestic problems of the society in which it lives. Arab antagonism is stimulated and sustained for reasons which have little to do, intrinsically, with Israel itself. For their own reasons, key groups in the Arab world wish to maintain the state of war with Israel. They need the war and therefore they will not end it; and most probably, as long as revolutionary changes threaten and beset the Arab states, the need will continue.

Ultimately, however, as the process of Arab national and social transformation continues, basic stability in a new societal context, will come to the Middle East. Once the threat of internal upheaval is past, there will no longer be need for a scapegoat. At that point the present posture of hostility and intransigence of the

Arab states can be expected to dissolve, and compromises on the outstanding issues in the Arab-Israeli dispute can be implemented.

While the ultimate prospects for Arab-Israeli coexistence may be good, the immediate prognosis seems to indicate an indefinite continuation of hostilities. But though the Middle East today presents a basic threat to the peace of the world, the issues must not be confused. It should be clear that only the parties directly involved in a particular struggle can resolve it. Only the United States can meet the Soviet challenge, and in this way reduce the danger of a world conflagration. Only the Arabs can ultimately solve their own internal dilemmas —and in whatever form proves to be acceptable to them. Only the Palestinian Arabs and the Israelis can ultimately resolve their conflict in a form that will be meaningful and lasting for both peoples.

The danger is that the wrong issues will be settled by the wrong parties. It is dangerous to fight a proxy war, and equally dangerous to attempt to impose a proxy peace, and the world has witnessed both in the Middle East in recent months.

The solution to the Arab-Israeli conflict may well be a long-range goal. Great patience is required, as well as the realization that efforts to force a settlement, no matter how well-meaning, could actually prove to be counterproductive. The world may have to accept the fact that until the internal conflicts within the Arab world itself are resolved, the Arabs will not be ready

to make peace with Israel. Unpleasant though this fact
may be, it can be accepted if the proper conclusions
are drawn from the situation: first, that Israel must be
kept strong enough militarily to contain the Arab threat
until such time as the Arabs are ready to make peace,
and second, that the Great Powers must act effectively
to remove the Middle East from the global confrontation in which they are engaged. In this way, the danger
that the Middle East holds for the world as a whole could
be reduced, and the ultimate solutions to the problems
of the area could be allowed to evolve.

It is essential to realize that the very existence of
Israel and its staggering and continued successes have
been a traumatic experience for the Arabs, and something to which they have not yet been able to adjust.
The Arabs have been beset by turmoil and have been
trying to adjust themselves to the modern world's demands since the turn of the century. Nationalism,
engulfing the Arab world, led the Arabs to fault their
own weakness as the product of foreign rule and op-
pression. The triumph of the movement of national
independence for most of the Arab states came after
World War II. But with its triumph came the unpleasant realization that national liberation, without
social and economic transformation, could not solve
basic national or social problems.

The Arab states today are in the throes of social
upheaval, economic change and national reorientation,
and these conflicts and agonies are unceasing. There are

conflicting ideologies, antagonistic movements and opposing nationalist programs. The Arab states are contesting for power, competing for loyalties, and bitterly hostile to one another. The Arab world is witnessing the destruction of its traditional society and is suffering from countless problems in its uncertain path towards some new form of society. The creation of Israel, as a Jewish state, is a challenge to the national sensibilities of the Arab world at a time when it is still groping for the form its own national identity will take. Israel's emergence as a modern, Western state is a challenge to the sensibilities of the Arab states still seeking to find their own path to modernity. They are unable to destroy this challenge and unwilling to accept it.

By its very nature, modernization is a destabilizing process. An inevitable byproduct is great internal dissension and unrest, as the existing social and political structure is split and torn off, made vulnerable to groups competing for supremacy and power.

It is a truism that the ruling elite in any society seeks first and foremost to remain in power. The constant struggle with Israel has proved a useful tool to the present leadership of the Arab states as that leadership seeks to preserve its position in the face of rampant instability.

Hatred of Israel also serves as a unifying factor in this period when so many forces encourage confrontation and disintegration. The consequence of the struggle with Israel can be used to mask domestic fail-

ures, or to divert threatened revolution. These factors
are equally valid in all the Arab states, irrespective of
the social system in power.

In the traditonal Arab societies, the main interest is
to stave off the threatening revolution. King Faisal of
Saudi Arabia, thus, gives large sums of money to the
Palestinian guerrilla groups, although these groups pro-
claim themselves to be dedicated to solve revolution and
are openly contemptuous of the society he is trying to
preserve. Faisal knows, however, that as long as the
Palestinian guerrillas continue to focus all radical
interest on the destruction of Israel, they will not be
preoccupied with the overthrow of the Saudi regime.
Similarly, Faisal is ready to give money to Egypt to
enable it to continue the struggle with Israel. The longer
Egypt is involved with Israel, the less is the danger that
some form of Nasserism will threaten the internal stability of Saudi Arabia. The traditional societies then,
have a vested interest in keeping the conflict alive, lest
they be swept away in the social revolution which would
inevitably follow its conclusion.

For the so-called radical states, the problem is more
complex. It is relatively easy for groups seeking change
in the traditonal states to identify all societal ills with
the ruling class and to be convinced that overthrowing
the existing social order would automatically result in
the necessary basic changes. But in many countries the
"revolution" occurred, changes were made, and still the
basic problems remained. The radical states thus face

the problem of satisfying the expectations which their revolutions awakened but have not been able to fulfill. President Nasser, after several years of attempted reform in Egypt, embarked on a program of foreign adventurism, Pan-Arabism and war with Israel. His purpose was, in part, to divert the attention of his people from the unfulfilled hopes of the revolution, in part to seek control of the oil-rich lands in order to gain the financial resources necessary for the modernization of Egypt, in part to find a scapegoat for his failures. Israel still serves as such a scapegoat for the radical states, which are beset with the danger of still further revolution.

Israel, in short, serves to maintain the power of the existing elites in both inter-Arab and intra-Arab disputes. She then must pay the price for the instability of the Arab world in whose midst she finds herself, and the price is to live in a constant state of war.

Underdeveloped countries are not only extremely conscious of their own instabilities, but hypersensitive to any allusion of their inferiority to the more developed nations of the world. They have a great need to reassert constantly their status of full equality in the world of modern nation states. This phenomenon is, to an extent, universal. Many have noted the seeming impropriety of the new states of Africa and Asia which have limited sources of income but which nonetheless spend large sums on questionable projects, such as national airlines or government buildings or chauffeured limousines for their officials. Yet these projects serve to bolster their self-esteem and symbolize their equality to the other nations. The Arabs tend to have the same sensitivity, perhaps particularly so because they are a great people with a great history and a justifiable sense of pride in their past glory. They feel bitter towards the West in general, on whose past imperialist rule and present economic exploitation they blame their backwardness. Much like other underdeveloped peoples, they relish any opportunity to show their strength vis-á-vis the Great Powers, and react negatively to any indication of the inherent weakness of their present situation.

This is why the Arab world was so pleased when Nasser "told off" the United States. All Arabs could hold their heads higher when the President of the U.A.R. informed the American government that it could "keep its aid." Similarly all Arabs could vicariously participate in the thrill of seeing Nasser playing off the Great Powers against one another throughout the late 50s and early 60s. Not Nasser alone, but all Arabs rose in their own esteem at the sight of the major world leaders arriving to woo the mighty Nasser. The central role of Nasser in the nonaligned bloc also was noted. While much of this might have been just show, the show itself was important. It was important psychologically.

Equally important to the Arabs is the necessity of avoiding any indication of their real weakness and backwardness. Israel, by its very success, is a constant humiliation, a constant reminder of what the Arabs are not—in spite of all their hopes, in spite of all their dreams, in spite of all their pretenses and in spite of all the self-deception and self-delusions. Israel is a scar upon their self-esteem which they cannot erase and, therefore, they pretend it does not really exist. For this reason the Arabs have made such an important point of ascribing Israel's military victories to Great Power intervention: Soviet support in 1948-49, British and French intervention in 1956, and the great hoax of the U.S. Air Force intervention in 1967. If the Great Powers had really been involved, then the Arab defeats would be understandable. To the Arabs, public acceptance of defeat by Israel would, of necessity, be public confession of basic weakness—and they cannot psychologically overcome this barrier.

In the same vein, the Arabs make a great issue of stating they will not negotiate while their land is occupied. Of course, as many have indicated, this is precisely the normal pattern of behavior, followed throughout history, whenever the armed forces of one state defeat those of another. However, if the Arabs succeed (as so far they evidently have) in not negotiating directly with Israel, then they can continue to maintain they were not defeated.

Arab obsession with self-image is still crucial. Israel, by its physical existence, simply does not allow the Arabs to live in the dream world to which they have become accustomed. It is a constant reminder of the real world, a world that is too painful for the Arabs to acknowledge. Every Israeli success is an Arab humiliation. Israel has drained the swamps, irrigated the deserts, industrialized the land and educated the people. The Arabs, faced with these same problems, have not been so successful in resolving them. It is so much easier to try to explain away Israel's success than to recognize Arab weakness.

The Arabs are bitter about their fate and frustrated by their inability to solve the profound problems which beset them. They fear the West, yet stand in awe of its technology, power, and achievements. To them, Israel represents the West. The Arabs wish to be modern and yet are afraid of losing their unique identity if they modernize. And Israel represents modernity personified, and with a unique identity as well. Israel represents, in short, much of what the Arabs aspire to become, are afraid of becoming, wish to become, and do not know how to become.

The Arabs have constructed a terrible image of Israel: It has been made the focus of all the fears and frustrations which beset the Arab people. As their difficulties and frustrations grow, so does their antagonism toward the Jewish state. To many Arabs, Israel has become the epitome of their own inferiority, the symbol of their discontent, and the cause of all their problems. Too many have made of Israel a test, identifying self-esteem and global equality with their ability to destroy the symbol of their current misfortunes—Israel.

Therefore, the Arabs do not wish to recognize Israel

—or to negotiate directly, or to sign a peace treaty, or to reach any kind of meaningful settlement. They view such a process as the ultimate humiliation and as the unveiling of their own weakness. The danger to the Arab states is not Israel itself but what they have made Israel represent.

With the modernization of the Arab world will come economic changes that will enable the Arabs to meet the needs of their own peoples. When the Arabs have solved their own problems, they will no longer need to resent the achievements of Israel. When their own self-image is raised, they will no longer feel inferior to Israel—or envious. Not long ago a leading advisor to Nasser indicated that even if all the political problems between Israel and the U.A.R. were settled, there still could not be normal relations between the two countries. Why? Because given Israel's economic and technological superiority, it could easily dominate the Arab world. When the time comes that the Arabs are secure enough in their own ability to withstand peaceful competition with Israel, such fears will no longer exist.

When Arab nationalism has reached its full development and a new form of Arab national entity is created, the Arabs will no longer see Israel as a threat to their own identity as Arabs. It is too early to foretell whether Pan-Arabism will triumph with one united Arab State, or whether the alliance between the U.A.R., Libya, and Sudan will turn into a new union, or whether a Fertile Crescent state will emerge. As long as Arab

nationalism is in flux, Israel is seen as a major block
to the achievement of Arab unity. If the Egyptian claim
to Arab leadership is stabilized, then Israel will no
longer appear as a threat to Egypt's ambitions in the
eastern half of the Arab world. Once the Arab national
revolution has run its course, then Israel will sink back
to its true perspective: a small piece of territory in the
vast Arab sea.

Until the time comes when Israel no longer is a
symbol to the Arabs but just a country, no solution
is really possible to the Arab-Israeli dispute. All the
world can do is try to defuse the danger which this
dispute entails. Israel must be kept militarily strong so
the Arab states cannot destroy her; Israel must be kept
viable until the time comes when the Arabs no longer
need to destroy her.

In recent years the growth of Palestinian nationalism
has added a new and complicating dimension to the
problem. For 20 years the Arab states used the Palestinians as a pawn in their battle with Israel. The defeat
of 1967 led to action by Palestinians independent of and
in some cases contrary to the wishes of the host Arab
states in which they lived. Whether Palestinian nationalism need have evolved at all is questionable. Had the
Arab states treated the population displaced by the
1948-49 war with the magnanimity that might have
been expected, the problem of the refugees could have
been solved with the integration of these people among
the Arabs in the U.A.R., Jordan, Syria, Lebanon, and/or

Iraq. By keeping them separate, by using them as political pawns, and fostering hatred of Israel among them, the Arab states have become the midwives of a unique Palestinianism. Today there is a Palestinian nationality which demands its self-determination and its own homeland. Most probably this demand for self-determination is as much a reaction against other Arabs who did not accept them as equals as it is against Israelis whom they blame for their homelessness.

In spite of the seemingly intractable problem of two peoples claiming the same land, the problem of the Palestinians could also be solved if there were readiness to seek a true solution, rather than to make use of the difficult situation. Mandated Palestine comprised all the land of present day Israel and Jordan and most of the territory occupied by Israel in the 1967 war. The Arab refugees have not lost their homeland—there never was a Palestine. An Arab Palestine was envisioned in the partition plan of 1947. Arab opposition to this plan precluded this state from being created. Actually, the vast majority of the Palestinians today are still living in Palestine. Many of them have merely, in fact, moved from one section of former Palestinian territory to another—some within the West Bank, some from one side of the Jordan to another. All this territory can, however, be considered part of the "Palestinian homeland." If the readiness existed, there would be a possibility of creating an Arab Palestine in addition to a State of Israel. The problem remains that no responsible

Palestinian leadership has evolved to give expression to the aspirations of the people. The guerrilla groups, to date the only meaningful exponent of Palestinian nationalism, demand the elimination of the State of Israel. When Palestinian leaders evolve who are ready to accept a solution that is reasonable although less than their total demands, a territorial compromise can be reached between Israel and the new Palestine. As long as Palestinian nationalism remains only in an extremist form its demands can never be achieved. It serves only to exacerbate an already difficult problem. Almost all the nationalist movements in history have had to compromise on their maximalist demands in order to realize and legitimize their national aspirations. This was true of Jewish nationalism, and it will one day be true of Palestinian nationalism.

But here again, only time and change will lead to the necessary results, which are a prerequisite for coexistence and peace in the Middle East.

The Arabs need and want to live in a world of illusion, maintaining their stance of hatred of Israel and perpetuating their hostility. It is only, however, the actions of the Soviet Union that have enabled the Arabs to continue this policy. Without the intervention of the Soviet Union, the Arabs would long since have had to come to terms with the reality of the Jewish state in their midst.

A differentiation must be made between the goal of the Soviet Union in the Middle East and the means and tactics it is using to achieve this goal. The Soviet Union exploits the Arab states' resentment of the West, and enjoys the fruits of Arab hatred of years of colonial misrule and economic exploitation. The rising Arab intelligentsia is especially bitter about this exploitation. The Arabs also blame the West for "imposing Israel on them" and for supporting the Israel which to them is so disastrous a symbol. The Soviet Union makes use of this antipathy, but the Arab-Israeli conflict is only a means to a much greater end: control of the entire Middle East and, through that control, a radical shift in the world balance of power.

The Soviet Union is, in fact, following the traditional pattern that other great powers have utilized. For 30 years, Great Britain made use of Arab-Jewish conflict in Palestine to maintain and strengthen its position in the Middle East. French policy, dating back to before the 1967 war, has been to support the Arab states as a way of ensuring increased French influence in an area from which France had been effectively eliminated. None of the Great Powers has operated in this area from pure motives, and the nations of the Middle East have suffered from the fact that each of the Great Powers has made use of the Middle East and its problems for its own selfish ends. Certainly today the problems are exacerbated by their involvement. The best solution for the Middle East, though unfortunately an illusory one, would be for the Great Powers to withdraw from the Middle East. Since such an eventuality is unlikely, it can be understood that the Soviet Union, as any other Great Power, would seek to achieve its own national interest to the greatest extent possible.

Only recently it might have been argued that the basic goal of Soviet policy was primarily defensive: to get the West out of areas where it has been well entrenched and to keep the West out of areas where it has already been expelled. It now seems clear, however, that the Soviet Union has embarked upon a strategy that seeks preeminence for itself in this area. As a result of its present politics it could gain further control in some of the radical Arab states, perhaps even leading to eventual sovietization. The Soviet Union could further the radicalization of some Arab states (Jordan and Lebanon) and work towards the overthrow of those states which are still basically pro-Western (Saudi Arabia and Kuwait). Continuing to make use of the Arab-Israeli dispute, with all the turmoil and social unrest rampant in the Arab world, the Soviet Union hopes to bring about the eventual elimination of all Western influence in the Middle East and replace it with Soviet-supported regimes.

Should this goal be achieved and the Soviet Union attain effective control of the Middle East, it would then be in a greatly strengthened strategic position in global terms. Europe would be outflanked and the U.S. Sixth Fleet placed in a most untenable position. The Soviet Union would be able to exert political blackmail on Western Europe and Japan, both of which are dependent on Middle East oil. Effective neutralization of these areas would result in the U.S. being forced to return to a "fortress America" concept, while the effective balance of power in the world would shift in favor of the Soviet Union.

Since the stakes are high, it should be understood, that the Arab-Israeli dispute is of vital interest to the Soviet Union. However, the Soviet Union has no intrinsic interest in the merits of the dispute itself, only in prolonging it indefinitely. It should also be noted in passing that while the Soviet Union is not really interested in the destruction of Israel (since this would remove a major cause of Arab antipathy to the West) it might well be prepared to tolerate such an eventuality if this would further its policy of seeking basic control of the entire Middle East.

Hitherto, the balance of power in the world has rested, since the end of World War II, on the knowledge that each of the two Great Powers would be prepared to act if the fundamental balance were challenged. Today, the Soviet Union is embarked upon precisely such a fundamental challenge in the Middle East. President Nixon's statement of July 1, 1970 seemed to indicate that the administration recognized the challenge. However, American policy in the past year has not been consistent with such recognition, and Soviet policy seems to have been predicated on the assumption that the United States was so involved in Vietnam and so torn with internal tensions that it would not stand

firm in the Middle East. America's hesitancy in supplying arms to Israel, as one example, has seemed to confirm
such an analysis.

In fact, the Soviet government could easily have
interpreted American policy as seeking to avoid a confrontation *at all costs.* If a global confrontation is to
be avoided, clear and direct action by the United States
must be taken to convince the Soviet Union that we
will not, as President Nixon has indicated, allow the
Soviet Union to achieve complete domination in the
Middle East. The issue has really nothing to do with
the Arab-Israeli dispute as such. The Soviet Union, as
it has done periodically since World War II, is seeking
control of an area basic to vital U.S. interests. Continuation of an indecisive U.S. policy in the Middle East
may well lead to an immediate disaster for Israel, but
the ultimate disaster will be to the United States and
to the peace of the world.

The Soviet Union has made such good use of the
Arab-Israeli dispute because it has no natural links that
would enable it to establish effective ties with the Arab
world. The natural trading partners of the Arabs are
in the West. The Soviet Union is an oil and cotton
exporting nation and, therefore, it does not really need
the commodities which are the leading products of the
Middle East. Its ties to the Arab world, then, are actually an economic liability. The Arab states need technological assistance to help them overcome the problems
inherent in the struggle for modernization. They would

prefer to deal with the West, which has more to offer them in terms of such assistance. Since the West needs what the Arabs produce and has what the Arabs want, logic would predict that close links would exist between the Arab world and the Western nations. It is only the Arab antipathy to the West and the existence of the Arab-Israeli dispute which enables the Soviet Union to overcome these natural drawbacks and establish effective ties with the Arab states.

Control of the Middle East has been a historic goal of the Russian state. For hundreds of years, Russian leaders have dreamed of reaching the Mediterranean and achieving warm water ports. Throughout the 19th century a prime objective in British foreign policy was to block Russia from this goal. Through their relations with the Arab states, the Russians have now bypassed Constantinople and have finally achieved the goal of establishing themselves in the Mediterranean basin. Soviet policy, then, can be seen in part as a continuation of a basic trend which has existed over long periods of time.

In addition, Soviet Middle Eastern policy can be understood in terms of how it serves the defensive needs of the Soviet Union. After fighting two disastrous wars in which it lost almost 50 million people, the Soviet Union emerged from World War II determined that never again would its border lands be used as a staging area for potentially hostile forces, Eastern Europe was therefore secured. Communist victories in

China and Soviet establishment of North Korea served this purpose in Asia. Only in the Middle East did Russia fail, in the immediate aftermath of World War II, to eliminate potentially anti-Soviet regimes from along its borders.

Therefore, since World War II the main goal and major interest of the Soviet Union in the Middle East has been to eliminate the presence of the West and/or regimes which tolerate or authorize the Western presence in this area so vital to Russia's security. And Russian policy has been amazingly consistent in following this goal.

Thus, in 1947-48 Russia supported the establishment of the State of Israel as the best means to eliminate the British from Palestine. British Palestine, at that time, was the single greatest Western presence in the Middle East. Soon after, the Soviet Union shifted to an anti-Israel policy in order to get the British out of Egypt and to ingratiate itself with the Arab peoples.

There is nothing contradictory in this shift from a pro-Israel to a vehemently anti-Israel position. The goal was and remains the same—to eliminate the Western presence in the Middle East. The Soviet Union has followed and will follow whatever techniques are best suited to achieve this goal.

The United States, under the leadership of former Secretary of State John Foster Dulles, sought to replace Great Britain and, through the Baghdad Pact, to build up Iraq as an anti-communist bastion along the "northern tier." This was essential to his effort to bring the Middle East directly into the global policy of containing communism. It was logical for the Soviet Union to respond to this attempt to thwart its policy, this challenge to its vital security interests as it saw them. Establishing links with Nasser was the means selected for challenging Dulles' efforts. Given the history of Egyptian-Iraqi competition for supremacy among the Arabs and Egyptian efforts to remove vestiges of British domination, Nasser was receptive to the Soviet attempt. Soviet arms cemented the relationship—thus, the only lasting contribution of the Dulles policy in the Middle East was to make it a major front of the cold war. It has become an increasingly important and volatile front of this war ever since.

Since their main interest is in keeping the West out, the Soviet Union is prepared to support anti-Western governments even if they are not pro-Communist. The Soviet Union, as any great power, seeks to advance its own national interests. If these interests coincide with the interests of international communism, that is an additonal benefit. However, the national interests of the Soviet Union are predominant. There are other examples of the Soviet Union's support of regimes which take militant action against local communist parties. The primary goal of Soviet policy in the Middle East today is not to install communist parties in power, but rather to remove any Western influence and to eliminate the possibility of the return of the West to this area. This goal can best be served by supporting and assisting radical regimes in several of the Arab states.

For the past 15 years Soviet policy in the Middle East has met with great success. This, however, is due as much to the reaction of the West to the Soviet policy as it is to any action the Soviet Union has taken. The West has supported the traditional elites in too many Arab states and, therefore, has become overly identified with old regimes which must be changed if the aspirations of the Arab peoples are to be achieved. The economic exploitation of the Arabs, with oil companies taking a disproportionate share of the wealth for their own profit, has furthered this antipathy. Finally, in the Arab-Israeli dispute the West has been identified with the State of Israel, which the Arabs have made the symbol of their own weakness and humiliation. And, interestingly enough, the Soviet Union has succeeded in making most of the Arabs forget that it, even more than the United States, supported the establishment of the State of Israel.

Since the Arab-Israeli dispute remains today the single greatest means by which the Soviet Union strengthens its own position, it has no interest in ending the conflict. Should the Arab-Israeli dispute be resolved, much of the Arab antipathy to the West might dissolve. This would result in increased trade between the Arabs and the West and in strengthened ties. Soviet influence would be limited and Soviet hopes of eliminating the West would be blocked. The Soviet Union must fear that a large-scale return of Western influence would doom to failure its entire policy of the last 25 years. Peace between Israel and the Arab states, then, would go directly against the vital interests of the Soviet Union as it defines them.

Only two factors might force the Soviet Union to change its policy and give up the great gains which it foresees. The first would be firm American action, since the Soviet Union wishes to avoid a nuclear confrontation. It must be emphasized, however, that American policy to date has not indicated that degree of firmness which would cause the Soviet Union to believe that America is prepared to act, if necessary, to prevent further Soviet expansion.

A second factor that might change Soviet policy could arise out of the potential threat of China. Communist China has been making efforts to gain control over the Palestinian guerrillas. Should the guerrillas become effective Chinese agents and begin to pose a real threat to the existing Arab regimes upon whose survival the Soviet influence rests, then the Middle East might become a Chinese sphere and the southern flank of the Soviet Union would be endangered. Therefore, the Soviet Union is interested in limiting the effectiveness of the guerrillas, to the extent that they can be controlled by the Arab states. Should the guerrilla movement become a real threat to the Arab regimes (except for Jordan, in whose survival the Soviet Union has no basic interest), then the Soviet Union might act to stabilize the situation before these regimes collapsed and Soviet influence with it.

If the United States were to act correctly, the same kind of balance between the Great Powers could be established in the Middle East as has been established in Europe, and the danger of global conflagration eliminated. The Soviet Union and the United States are conducting two-power talks on the Middle East, which is good. But unfortunately, they are talking about the wrong subjects. The United States and the Soviet Union can only effectively agree upon issues which they control. They should be discussing a guarantee of non-involvement in any new Arab-Israeli conflict, since that is what they are most concerned about. They might also discuss means of stabilizing the Arab-Israeli conflict until such time as the Soviet Union would be prepared to use its influence to encourage a meaningful settlement. If the danger is the escalation of the Arab-Israeli dispute into a Great Power confrontation then this is the danger that has to be met. Any attempt to force a solution of the Arab-Israeli dispute itself would, of necessity, be doomed to failure, since only a basic change in the Arab attitude would permit such a solution.

The realistic options, then, allow us to outline an American policy which would signal the Soviet Union that the United States is prepared to meet the challenge which the Soviet bid for supremacy portends. Once this is done, Israel should be kept militarily strong enough to offset the Arab threat until such time as the Arabs are prepared to live in peace.

As to specifics, it serves little purpose to talk at length about various possible ways of solving the outstanding issues of the Arab-Israeli dispute. Most of the issues could easily be resolved if there were readiness to seek solutions.

The question of Israel's security, for example, could be solved through demilitarization of the Sinai and some special arrangements for the Sharm al Sheikh. The Golan heights could be effectively demilitarized. Most of the West Bank could be returned. A new state might be established, either instead of or in additon to the existing state of Jordan, in order to satisfy the national aspirations of the Palestinian people. Given human ingenuity, arrangements could be made to maintain the unity of Jerusalem (which nobody wants divided again) —and still provide for the religious interests concerned with the city. The refugee problem could be solved through the repatriation of some and the resettlement of others, all within the borders of what was once Palestine. These issues, as already indicated, are but a reflection of the Arab-Israeli dispute and not its cause. When the Arabs are prepared to live at peace with Israel, these problems will be settled. It might also be noted that the United Nations can play only a limited role in any such settlement. When the Arabs are prepared to live with Israel, the two sides will not need the United Nations to bring them together. And as long as the Arabs are not prepared to live with Israel, no army the United Nations can form is large enough to make them do so.

It also serves little purpose to wax euphoric over the great potential which lies in wait for the nations of the Middle East once peace is attained. It is true that economic relations, scientific exchange and various kinds of technical assistance among the nations of the Middle East would be of great benefit to all the peoples of the area. Similarly, one day, there might be economic confederation and perhaps even political confederation, involving Israel and the Arab states. Only time, however, can bring this about.

To talk of a binational state is the height of ludicrousness. In the best of cases, there are tremendous problems in any binational state. Given the animosity and mistrust which the Arab-Israeli dispute has engendered, a binational state is simply impossible. The truth is, also, that the only binational state the Arabs would be ready to accept is one in which the Jews were second-class citizens in an Arab Palestine. This is the meaning of the "democratic secular Palestine" that the Arab guerrillas have been espousing. It is a guise behind which large numbers of Jews would be eliminated and the remnants would remain as a "tolerated" minority in an Arab land. The Arab peoples, like so many other peoples, have suffered from a by-product of nationalism —the mistreatment of national and religious minorities. Whatever the ultimate relations between the Israelis and Arabs in the Middle East, be they political, economic or cultural, they will be meaningful only to the extent that they come about as the culmination of a natural process of evolution. They cannot be imposed from outside.

The Middle East is beset by many complex problems. Attempts at forcing solutions to these problems, no matter how well meaning, could be disastrous. Only the parties to the conflict can solve the issues of the conflict. Only the United States can meet the challenge of the Soviet Union. Only the Arabs can solve the problems which beset them in a way which they would accept. Only the Arabs and the Israelis can solve the problems which concern them. The world must learn that certain problems may prove to be insoluable and that, therefore, the dangers which these problems present to the world must be avoided while the search for long-term solutions continues. This will no doubt be the fate of the Arab-Israeli dispute. It can and must be defused and stabilized. But only with time and basic changes can it be truly solved.

FOURTH LECTURE

CHRISTOPHER MAYHEW

The dangers of the Arab-Israeli struggle can hardly be exaggerated. They are widely understood and need no elaboration. The most imaginative writer could hardly hope to invent a scenario more fraught with peril to mankind.

It is unfortunately too much to hope that any settlement can be reached which would quickly end all acts of violence between Israelis and Palestinian Arabs. This paper simply attempts to set out, as realistically as possible, the course of action which the writer feels has the best chance—albeit a slender one—of limiting the scale of violence and of doing as much justice as possible to the interests and the aspirations of the protagonists.

The *interests* of the Israelis and the Palestinian Arabs are reconcilable—at least on paper. But the *objectives* which they are currently pursuing, passionately and implacably, are not. We should therefore, perhaps, start by considering these objectives and examining how far the two sides can be induced to modify them in order to limit the scale of violence between them. This would automatically reduce the sharpness of the Great Power

confrontation in the region, and lessen the likelihood
of the conflict escalating into world war.

I. The Demands of the Palestinian Arabs

The principal objective of the main body of the
Palestinian resistance movement is the creation of an
independent, democratic, sovereign state in all of Palestine. The "legitimate inhabitants" of Palestine would
share equal rights, irrespective of religion or language.
"Legitimate inhabitants" include all Jews who lived in
Palestine during the Mandate and their descendants,
and all Jews now living in Israel who are prepared to
renounce Zionism and live in a liberated Palestine,
forming part of the Arab homeland.

This conception of a united, multiracial Palestine,
in which Arabs and Jews coexist peacefully is attractive
in principle, and has a wide appeal to that part of
world opinion—perhaps the largest part—which does
not understand, or rejects, Zionist ideas. There is no
reason to suppose that the Palestinian Arabs will ever
abandon this deeply felt aspiration, even if they have
no real prospect of achieving it, and even if they cease
actively pursuing it. Their claim that Palestine belongs
to the Arabs is at least as deeply felt (and in the view
of the writer has at least as much validity in terms of
history and natural justice), as the claim of Zionists
that Palestine belongs to the Jews. Arab Zionism is likely
to be as enduring as Jewish Zionism, and must be

expected to persist, at least in the form of a romantic yearning, for centuries.

The parallels between Arab and Jewish Zionism are numerous, and are increasing. Conversations with Palestinian refugees today—whether in the camps, in Israeli-occupied territories, or in the many far-flung places throughout the world where Palestinians now reside—bear an extraordinary resemblance to conversations with Jewish refugees during their dark days of the thirties. "Palestine belongs to us. No matter how long we have to wait, no matter what sacrifices we have to make, we shall return." A literature of Arab Zionism is growing, markedly similar to the literature of Jewish Zionism. *The Times* of London recently quoted a good example from Nashashibi's "Return Ticket":

> Every year I shall say to my little son, "We shall return, my son, and you will be with me; we shall return to our land and walk there barefoot. We will remove our shoes so that we may feel the holiness of the ground beneath us. . . . Do you not remember Jaffa and its delightful shore, Haifa and its lofty mountain . . . the streets of Jerusalem, my dear Jerusalem, Tiberias and its peaceful shore with the golden waves . . . ?"

And so on.

It is a terrible truth that the Palestinian Arabs have now been dispersed from Palestine by the Jews, much as the Jews were dispersed from Palestine by the Romans, and that their reactions are likely to be just as passionate and enduring. Indeed, the Palestinian Arabs can be expected to feel their loss even more acutely inasmuch as their ties with Palestine are personal as well as racial and national—and also more recent, more immediate, and more obviously unchallengeable.

Nevertheless, however understandable—and however attractive in principle—the Palestinians' objective of a united multiracial Palestine may be, it is plainly not practicable. Even on the extreme assumption of a collapse of Israeli power, a *multiracial* Palestine would not be a likely outcome. It is unrealistic to suppose that those Israelis who had managed to survive the preceding desperate holocaust would consent to participate afterwards in a multiracial experiment with their Arab conquerors. Given a victory for Arab arms, it is possible to envisage a united *Arab* Palestine, but not a Palestine in which Arabs and Jews coexist peacefully. Nor is it realistic to assume that the dismantling of the State of Israel would be acceptable to the United States and other outside powers, including the Soviet Union, which steadily continues to insist on Israel's right to survive as a state.

We therefore have to face the fact that, for an indefinite period, large numbers of Palestinian Arabs will continue passionately attached to an objective which cannot be achieved. And we must assume that at least a small minority of them will continue for an indefinite period to fight for this objective by violent means. Meanwhile, no peace in the region is possible while Palestinian Arabs continue to insist on, and to back with force, the full implementation of their objective of a united multiracial Palestine.

This does not mean, however, that the Palestinians' aspirations can be ignored and their resistance suppressed. They are a talented, vigorous people; they have been treated abominably; their feelings of frustration and humiliation are natural and human; and they have a growing number of powerful friends. Unless they are given some substantial satisfaction of their demands, it would not be practicable—or just—to attempt to coerce them into acquiescing in a settlement.

It is therefore necessary to go to the limits of what is practicable to meet their aspirations.

Two lines of approach suggest themselves. The first is the encouragement of the idea of an independent sovereign Palestinian state in the Arab territories at present occupied by Israel. These territories unfortunately constitute a very awkward entity, geographically and economically (even if extra-territorial rights were given to the new state in a corridor between Gaza and the West Bank). Yet if as a result of a peace settlement the occupied Arab territories were liberated, it is possible that as the Israeli troops withdrew—whatever claims to control are made by the United Nations or by the Jordan army—the Palestinian resistance organizations would in practice find themselves the de facto authorities on the spot. Provided they maintain sufficient unity among themselves, these organizations would be in a position to establish a government and win interna-

tional recognition. The inhabitants of the new state
could be given an opportunity, if they wished, to form
a federal relationship with Jordan. All the 1967 Arab
refugees could be, and no doubt would be, welcomed
back to their old homes.

This "half loaf" solution is at present rejected outright by the Palestine Liberation Organization. But it
is by no means certain that in this rejection—or indeed
in their opposition to the Rogers proposals—the resistance movements and their leaders speak for the bulk
of Palestinian Arabs in the occupied territories. In the
circumstances of an Israeli withdrawal, the opposition
of a large number of Palestinian Arabs to the "half
loaf" solution might well evaporate. Although it would
neither be just nor practicable to require Palestinian
Arabs to abandon their ultimate hope of a united
Palestine—which could, in any case, possibly result
from a long-term process of de-Zionization within
Israel—this half-way solution might be sufficiently
acceptable to a sufficient number of Palestinians to
keep conflict within manageable limits, so that a settlement (on the lines of Resolution 242) would become
viable. The Lebanese, Jordanians, and Egyptians would
have no wish to upset such a settlement, and the Syrians
and Iraqis would not have the power to do so.

Nevertheless, the establishment of this minimal Arab
Palestinian state would not be enough. A long overdue
act of justice needs to be done to the 1948 Arab refugees. They must be given the right, accorded to them

in repeated, unanimous resolutions of the UN General Assembly, to choose between repatriation to Israel or compensation and resettlement elsewhere. In the circumstances of the territorial settlement now envisaged, a high proportion of these refugees would probably elect for compensation and resettlement—many of them, no doubt, in the new Arab state. Few would wish to return to live in a specifically Jewish state. Nevertheless it is essential that the refugees' right to return should be asserted, and in practice this should not present an unacceptable security or administrative problem for the Israelis.

II. The Demands of Egypt and Jordan

Like all Arabs, President Nasser and King Hussein are passionately anti-Zionist and would no doubt be happy to see the State of Israel dismantled. But this is not their objective. They are realists. They know that the idea of a united, multiracial Palestine is impracticable, and since 1967 they have consistently worked for, and publicly supported, the implementation of the UN Security Council Resolution number 242. One of the most important successes of Zionist propaganda during this period has been to mislead western opinion on this point. In particular the widespread belief in many Western countries that President Nasser aimed at "driving the Israelis into the sea"—even that he had said so publicly—has been of considerable value to Israeli foreign policy. In retrospect it is easy to see

that this was a serious misjudgment. Nasser's unconditional acceptance of the Rogers proposals and of the
cease-fire on the Suez Canal did not constitute a change
of policy. But since it entailed specific public actions—
notably the ending of hostilities on the Suez Canal—it
put the position of the U.A.R. government beyond the
possibility of misrepresentation.

The principal aim of the Jordanian and U.A.R. governments is to secure the evacuation of all their territories by Israel. They have, however, conceded that they
would be willing to consider frontier "rectifications"
in a settlement. By this they envisage the yielding of
small areas on the frontiers in return for an accession
of small areas elsewhere. They would find it impossible
to accept any proposals involving a net loss of Arab
territories to Israel.

King Hussein has stated that, in the event of Israel's
withdrawal from the West Bank, he would wish a
formal assertion of Jordanian sovereignty to be made
over these territories but that, thereafter, the inhabitants would be free to determine their own future. He
has publicly acknowledged that if the Palestinian Arabs
choose to detach themselves from Jordan, they may
do so with his goodwill.

The Egyptians have made no public statement about
the future of Gaza in the event of Israeli withdrawal,
but they would certainly not wish to reassert any rights
for themselves in that territory.

Thus the territorial demands of the Jordanian and

U.A.R. governments are clearly defined. Moreover, they are reconcilable with Resolution 242 if this is interpreted —as U.S. Secretary of State Rogers interpreted it in presenting his earlier peace proposals last year—as requiring Israeli withdrawal from conquered Arab territories to the 1967 frontiers, with only "insubstantial" changes "not reflecting the weight of conquest." Besides these territorial demands, the two governments also require the Arab refugees to be offered a choice of repatriation to Israel, or of compensation and resettlement elsewhere, a point which has already been dealt with above.

In short, the position of the two governments is fully in line with the Rogers proposals and Resolution 242, and if these were similarly acceptable to the Palestinian Arabs and the Israelis, there would be little difficulty in reaching a peaceful settlement. The obstacles do not come from the Jordanian or U.A.R. governments. On the contrary, hopes for a peaceful settlement rest on the continuance of these governments in power, and their maintenance of their present policies.

At the time of writing, no evidence is publicly available that the Egyptians have deliberately broken the cease-fire agreement. This agreement, incidentally, is open to misinterpretation, especially in relation to the movement of missile sites *within* (not *into*) the cease-fire zone. Israel's allegations of deliberate violations of the cease-fire may turn out to be well-founded. But such violations by President Nasser would appear to be wholly irrational in the light of his acceptance of the Rogers proposals, which was widely welcomed in the Arab world as a diplomatic out-flanking of the Israelis. There is a real possibility, moreover, that the Israeli government was anxiously looking for a pretext for withdrawing from negotiations which she had agreed to undertake only after long and difficult deliberation.

Other Arab governments, notably Syria, Iraq, and Algeria, have of course declared their outright opposition to the Rogers proposals and Resolution 242, and their support for the Palestinian demand for a united, multiracial Palestine. But these governments are not in a position to prevent a settlement if the Jordanian and U.A.R. governments stand firm, and if the settlement offers sufficient satisfaction to a sufficient proportion of the Palestinians.

III. The Objectives of Israel

A significant proportion of Israeli opinion—in particular that part led by the right-wing Gahal party—is avowedly expansionist. It opposes withdrawal from occupied Arab territories, and indeed, in some cases, demands further expansion of Israel's borders. Most Israelis approve of the establishment of permanent Jewish settlements on the West Bank, and of the erection of public buildings and residential blocks for Jewish people in east Jerusalem. Almost all Israeli opinion favors new mass immigration of Jewish people into Israel.

The overriding Israeli demand, however, is for security. This is a fact which the Arabs naturally find it hard to accept. Their knowledge of Zionism is primarily based on their first-hand experience of being invaded, overrun, and bombed—of having their own security destroyed. But no one who visits Israel and talks to the Israelis can doubt that the overwhelming majority of them would be willing to make considerable concessions if they believed that this would increase their security.

Unfortunately, however, the Israelis' judgment of their own security interests has been extremely short-sighted. On several occasions since 1948 it would have been possible for them, with a greater degree of courage and statesmanship, to have established a modus vivendi with their Arab neighbors—especially, perhaps, in 1955 and 1967. By a tragic misjudgment, however, they have acted throughout on the assumption that their best chance of safety was to dominate their neighbors militarily, including—in 1967—seizing and holding tactically advantageous territory far beyond their own frontiers. Yet no country which occupies tens of thousands of square miles of its neighbors' territory (and rules over more than a million of their people with an increasingly heavy hand) can expect to live in peace, or indeed deserves to do so.

It is a sad feature of human nature that insecurity breeds aggressiveness. For historical reasons, which every civilized person understands and respects, the Jewish people are haunted by an almost pathological sense of insecurity. This leads them to seek power over their opponents in ways which, by a tragic paradox, create the very dangers they are so anxious to avoid. It is possible to say truthfully that Israel's overriding demand is for security, and also that the actions that she takes are aggressive and could ultimately prove self-destructive.

A peaceful settlement requires that Israel withdraw to her 1967 frontiers—with "insubstantial" changes. Yet, though this is her only chance of long-term security, her deeply-felt fears and suspicions inhibit her from seizing it. Hence her consistent opposition to all schemes for a settlement which involve, for example, withdrawal from Sharm al Sheikh, the Golan heights, and other strategically important places. Consequently, her demand to be allowed to live in peace, though sincere, sounds increasingly hollow—like the plea of a burglar to be left alone with his loot.

Since it is not primarily prompted by a desire for security, Israel's claim to maintain her exclusive control over the whole of Jerusalem arouses particularly wide opposition. The demand has been unanimously condemned by the General Assembly of the United Nations and by the Security Council. It has no basis in law, history, or natural justice, and is wholly incompatible with a peaceful settlement.

If Israel were to abandon her demand to retain Arab territory, then her other demands—for recognition, for a peace treaty, and for the freeing of international waterways—should present comparatively little difficulty. Moreover, when the 1967 Arab refugees have returned to the occupied Arab territories, a just settlement for the 1948 refugees should be negotiable on the lines discussed above.

This brief examination of the conflicting objectives of the Israelis and the Arabs suggests that no peaceful settlement is possible in the absence of strong external pressures on the participants. Left to themselves, the Israelis will not withdraw from the Arab territories; nor will the Arab governments accept an indefinite cease-fire; nor will the Palestinians desist from their violent resistance. In these circumstances, the future is fairly easy to predict. It presents a picture of disaster. The war would continue to escalate and casualties would continue to mount. Then, first the Russians, and afterwards the Americans, would find themselves faced with the agonizing choice between letting their protégés suffer and intervening ever more directly in their defense with their own armed forces.

IV. Objectives of the Great Powers

What prospect is there that the U.S. and Soviet governments can and will exert the pressures needed to reach a settlement?

Anti-Zionist propaganda pictures U.S. imperialism backing Israel in order to advance its strategic and economic interests in the Middle East. This is, of course, a caricature of American policy. But almost equally distorted is the pro-Zionist picture of the Soviet Union advancing its power and interests in the Middle East by manipulating its Arab satellites. The growth of Russian influence is of course unquestionable, but the motivation behind it is less positive and aggressive than is often painted. The provision of Soviet arms, technicians, and pilots to Egypt has been made with considerable reluctance—in response to fervent and repeated pleas from Nasser, arising from his inability to defend his own territory and people. The Russians certainly dislike making these deliveries, which are not only unremunerative, but lead them towards a closer, unwelcome confrontation with the United States. And the Egyptians certainly dislike having to ask for them, and thus putting themselves under an obligation to a power which the great majority of them dislike and distrust.

Soviet policy in the region is, in fact, a mass of contradictions. On the one hand, it supports Resolution 242, tacitly acquiesces in the Rogers proposals, and steadily affirms Israel's right to exist as a state. On the other hand, it arms—indirectly—a number of Palestinian groups aiming at the destruction of the State of Israel, and continues giving its traditional support to Communist elements in all Middle Eastern countries (including Israel) aiming at conventional Soviet-type revolution.

Judgment of overall Soviet objectives is therefore

extremely difficult. It may be that the Soviet Union's overriding aim is to avoid a confrontation with the United States at a time when its main fears are centered on the Chinese; and to prevent the Chinese from ousting the Russians as the Arabs' most influential supporters. On this hypothesis, Soviet leaders may judge that their best interests lie in a peaceful settlement on the lines of Resolution 242 and in neutralizing the Palestine Resistance Movement. It is reassuring that they have steadily and scrupulously refused to supply Egypt with offensive missiles or bombers capable of attacking Tel Aviv unlike—it must be said—the Americans, who have supplied Israel with offensive aircraft capable of attacking Cairo.

Since 1948, Israel has been militarily dominant in the region, so that the pressure on the Soviet Union to give direct military assistance to the Arabs has been much greater than the pressure on the United States to give similar assistance to Israel. When Cairo was at the mercy of the Phantoms, the pressure on the Soviet Union to provide Egypt with antiaircraft defense proved irresistible. If the balance of power changed, so that Tel Aviv became threatened by Soviet weapons, the pressure on the United States to act as the Russians have done would probably prove equally irresistible.

It is reasonable to assume that Israel's military domination will be maintained for several years to come, so that the United States will not be faced for some time with this Soviet dilemma. But, in the absence of a settlement, it seems quite likely that the balance of power will start shifting against the Israelis. It may be doing so already. When it does, the Americans will be faced with a decision even more momentous than the decision to fight in Vietnam.

Indeed, the Middle East conflict is already producing parallels with Vietnam. Some Arab extremists make crude but plausible comparisons along these lines. The Algerian leaders, for example, simply equate Palestine with Vietnam and Algeria: "Just as the American Asian puppet, South Vietnam, is being mastered by the Vietcong, so their Middle Eastern puppet, Israel, will succumb to the Palestinian resistance." Or they put it this way: "Just as the French colonial settlers in Algeria, backed by the French army, were eventually vanquished by the forces of Algerian liberation, so the Jewish colonial settlers in Palestine, backed by the Americans, will be beaten by the forces of Palestinian liberation."

These are of course absurd oversimplifications. But it is nevertheless true that if the Americans ever became compelled to intervene in the Middle East war, they would find themselves, as in Vietnam, supporting a small, westernized, anti-Communist ally against large, leftist, anti-colonial, "liberation" forces, supported by a large and vociferous section of world opinion.

What can be done to avert this forbidding prospect?

V. A Last Chance?

If the foregoing analysis of Israeli and Palestinian objectives is broadly correct, it follows that the Rogers proposals were well-judged and constructive, but that if they are to succeed, they require some supplementation. Otherwise the Israelis, haunted by their sense of insecurity, will not withdraw sufficiently to enable the Egyptian and Jordanian governments to deliver their side of the bargain. Nor will sufficient satisfaction be given to Palestinian aspirations to make the settlement enforceable and viable. An attempt must therefore be made to strengthen Israel's prospective security if and when she withdraws to her old frontiers; and the Palestinians must be given some satisfaction of their aspirations. Heavier pressure on both will also plainly be needed to induce them to conform.

What can be offered to Israel to increase her sense of security on her old frontiers? She herself attributes importance to the formal signing of a peace treaty, and there need be no difficulty about this provided that other parts of the Rogers proposals are fully implemented. It is difficult, however, to share Israel's faith in the value of written guarantees of this kind.

There is wide agreement that in the event of withdrawal there should be a demilitarized zone on both sides of the old frontier—perhaps averaging about 30 kilometers wide—manned by a UN peace-keeping force. This force could be withdrawn only by unanimous agreement of the Security Council, that is, with the consent of the Israeli and Arab governments. Israel has so far shown no interest in proposals of this kind. But if the prospects of a peaceful settlement became more immediate, so that Israel was forced to make a realistic assessment of her security requirements on her old frontiers (which her chiefs of staff do not appear to have done yet), this attitude might change.

The idea might be made more attractive to the Israelis if the potential fighting power of the proposed UN peace-keeping force were increased. Might it not include, for example, sizable contingents from France and Britain? These would make the UN force a good deal more credible and would enable it, if necessary, to call upon air and naval power from the eastern Mediterranean. There are good reasons for believing that despite its "neocolonial" appearance, a Franco-British contribution to the UN force would be acceptable to the U.A.R. and Jordanian governments, with whom the idea has been discussed informally. These governments could, and no doubt would, present the French and British presence as an extra safeguard to their own peoples against renewed Israeli expansion. If the idea were acceptable to these governments, and were part of the package deal envisaged in Resolution 242, there is a fair chance that the Russians would acquiesce in it. And the French and British governments could probably be persuaded to play their part, albeit reluctantly.

Senator William Fulbright has suggested that the United States should give an outright defense guarantee to Israel, undertaking to assist her with all measures necessary to overcome any threat which she found herself unable to handle unaided. This high degree of American involvement would be extremely unwelcome to the Arab and Soviet governments, and it would no doubt be strongly questioned by a substantial section of American opinion. It would plainly need to be matched by a parallel Soviet guarantee to the Arab governments, an involvement which would in its turn be highly unwelcome to the Israelis and to the United States.

This prospect of a Middle East dominated by the Great Powers, of an eyeball-to-eyeball confrontation between them across a disputed and uneasy frontier, is unattractive. It might therefore be preferable, at least in the first instance, to enlist the aid of medium-sized powers acting within the ambit of the United Nations and less closely committed to either side in the dispute.

A notable gap in the Rogers proposals was the absence of any inducement to the Palestine Resistance Movement to moderate its extreme demands. It is true that, if implemented, the proposals would enormously benefit Palestinian Arabs at present under Israeli occupation— and also the 1967 Arab refugees. But no concession is implied to the Palestinians' just and natural claim for some expression of their own national identity. An advance in this direction could be made if the governments concerned openly acknowledged the right of the Palestinians in Gaza, the West Bank, and east Jerusalem to form their own, independent, sovereign state if they so wished, and indicated their willingness to recognize such a state if it were formed.

If these two proposals, relating to Israel's security and Palestinian aspirations, were added to the Rogers proposals and to Resolution 242, the resulting package might conceivably constitute an enforceable, viable peace settlement. But the settlement could plainly not be agreed upon without a degree of pressure on both the Israelis and the Palestinians.

The Jordanian, Egyptian, and Soviet governments could be expected to do their best to induce the Palestinians to conform. (At the time of writing the Jordanian government is in armed conflict with militant Palestinians opposing a settlement.) Undoubtedly, the prospect not merely of liberation from Israeli rule, but of the establishment of an independent Palestinian Arab state would very greatly reduce popular support for guerrilla movements opposing the settlement.

The only government capable of bringing effective pressure on the Israelis is, of course, the United States government. And unfortunately the prospect of the necessary pressure being brought to bear is a doubtful one. Up to the time when the Rogers proposals were launched, the U.S. government continued sending the Israelis essential arms and equipment, even while they were flatly rejecting its own peace proposals; and there are some signs that this strange situation may be about to recur. If so, there seems to be no prospect of an Israeli withdrawal from the occupied Arab territories, and therefore no prospect of a peaceful settlement. The process of military escalation will be resumed, until the United States finds herself drawn into a new overseas war even more dangerous than the Vietnamese war, and even more damaging to herself.

VI. Conclusion

The outlook for peace is very bleak. The rays of hope lighted by the Rogers proposals have been dimmed by the terrorists of the Popular Front for the Liberation of Palestine, and by Israel's suspicion, which may or may not be justified, that the Egyptian and Soviet governments have been systematically violating the cease-fire provisions. But, at least, at the time of writing, fighting has not yet been resumed, and procedures have been broadly agreed upon for negotiations to take place. If the utmost efforts are made to reassure Israel about her security on her old frontiers, and if every possible step is taken to fulfill the achievable aspirations of the Palestinians, a faint hope of peace remains.

REBUTTALS

I. L. KENEN

I must say it's not a simple matter to answer both Rabbi Berger and Mr. Mayhew in five minutes.

Mr. Mayhew has put forward a somewhat bland picture of the threat to Israel at this time. I'd like to call your attention to his paper. It contains a very moving passage from Nashashibi's *Return Ticket* in which the author tells his young son about the holiness and beauties of Palestine and promises that some day they will return. For Mr. Mayhew this is Arab Zionism which, he says, is as enduring as Jewish Zionism. Incidentally, he seems to approve of Arab Zionism although his colleague, Dr. Berger, is so vehemently opposed to Jewish Zionism. But the reason I call attention to this is that Mr. Mayhew, and this is the crux of the matter, did not quote far enough. If he had turned the page and gone on to quote the rest of that poem, he would have read what the Arab father was saying about what is in the hearts of some of the Palestinians today:

> I shall see the hatred in the eyes of my son and your sons. I want them to be callous and to be ruthless. I want them to enter their lairs . . . we will enter their lairs in Tel Aviv. We will smash

Tel Aviv with axes, guns, hands, fingernails and teeth.

That is what they say. That is why we get only one half of the story in that serene picture which Mr. Mayhew has presented. I don't think Jewish Zionism ever taught its people to hate the Arabs.

The other statement to which I must take exception in the limited time I have has to do with the proposal that Israel offer Arabs repatriation. Looking across at what is happening in Amman today, Israelis will insist that repatriation means to export into the streets of Jerusalem, Haifa, and Tel Aviv the kind of ghastly blood bath which today drowns humanity in Jordan. Mr. Mayhew has told us the Russians have not provided Egypt with bombers or missiles to bomb Tel Aviv. That appears in his prepared statement. And here again, he gives the impression that the Russians are not really the kind of menace which Israel regards them to be. But he's apparently forgotten—I don't know how he came to make that statement—that over the years the Russians have provided Egypt with Tupelov-16 bombers, with Zukov-7s and IL-28s. In case you have forgotten, it was the presence of Illyushin 28s in Cuba to which President Kennedy took such sharp exception back in 1962. So I don't think we shall underestimate the menace which the Soviet Union today presents. It's interesting that neither Dr. Berger nor Mr. Mayhew referred at all to the missile buildup in the Suez area at this time.

If the Palestinian Arabs wanted to create their state in the West Bank and in Gaza and in East Jerusalem, they had 22 years or so in which to do it. One wonders why they didn't bring it into being in all that time. And, of course, the Palestinian Arabs can still create their own state if they want to take over Jordan and if they want to negotiate then with Israel for borders with respect to the West Bank. It is up to them.

The Palestinians were citizens of Jordan. They had a voice over its destiny. I would agree completely, Mr. Mayhew, that Israelis and Arabs will be able to understand each other better if they can talk to each other. That's why I am so insistent that there be direct talks at some stage, because only then will they begin to understand each other. And the fact of the matter is that the Arabs on the West Bank have come to understand the Israelis a great deal more and I don't think that those Arabs, no matter what happens, will want to see the sand curtain drop again between them and Israel. I think they will want some kind of continuing communication.

That's one of the hopeful aspects of the situation. But the kind of state which Mr. Mayhew was talking about is the kind of state which is opposed by the Palestinians whom I quoted earlier. What they are talking about is the liquidation of Israel and its replacement by something where Jews may live as they have lived nowhere else in the Arab world.

This is the point that I think we should understand.

Dr. Berger is not concerned too much about the plight
of the Jews in the Arab countries. There are very, very
few Jews left in the Arab countries today and those
who are left are anxious to get out. But there are more
than 300,000 Arabs inside Israel. Their living conditions
and their opportunities for advancement and education
are much better than those of the Jews living in Arab
countries today.

I won't take the time to argue with the irrelevant and
obsolete views that Dr. Berger presents here about the
Jewish people. His views have been repudiated, ever
since they were first promulgated, by an avalanche
of American Jewish opinion. He does not believe in
the Jewish people. Regrettably, however, he has become,
as he himself said in his statement, one of the ideologues
of the Palestinian Arab movement by giving them the
impression that there is no such concept as the Jewish
people—that the Jewish people have never existed in
the past and are not destined to exist in the future.
I suggest to you that most Jews devoutly believe in the
future of the Jewish people and are determined that
that people will continue to survive in the future.

ELMER BERGER

Knowing something about the semantics of this problem and knowing how much of a problem it has been in rational discussion, I think I ought to address myself for a moment to this question of "the Jewish people." I don't really know what the term means in its broad sense and it's quite obvious that there is a good deal of difference among Jews as to what it means. But there's one thing that I think no one has ever proven, despite what Mr. Kenen just said. And that is whether or not the majority of Jews throughout the world consider themselves to be a part of the Jewish people as a subject of international law—enjoying and wanting a system of functional nationality rights and obligations with respect to the State of Israel. I seriously doubt this is acceptable to the majority of Jews of the world, and Mr. Kenen knows as well as I do that this has been the essence of the debate among Jews with respect to Zionism and anti-Zionism ever since there has been a national Zionist movement.

Now beyond that, and in terms perhaps more directly relevant to the question tonight, it seems to me that

—like Mr. Kenen—there is very little I think necessary to add to my original statement.

It's quite obvious that Mr. Mayhew and I, on the one hand, and Dr. Pollack and Mr. Kenen, on the other, simply operate on different wave lengths. Both of the representatives or spokesmen or advocates of the Zionist/Israeli position appear to accept Israel's right to exist as unqualified and unconditional. But the facts are—and if law has any relationship to a just peace, which is the subject of the evening—the facts are that every single international agreement in support of any Zionist presence in Palestine always has explicitly limited this Zionist right by specifying the existing rights of the "non-Jewish people" nationals of Palestine.

And although less frequently specified in these agreements, Zionist/Israeli claims to sovereignty have also been limited by the rights and political status of Jews in any other country. The Zionist/Israeli establishment, with the indulgence of the Great Powers of the West, has consistently flouted both of these limitations. The chaos in the Middle East—including now the danger of total collapse in Jordan, with all that this may mean for all who have interests in the area—is a not unexpected consequence of the disintegration of any rule of law with respect to the Zionist establishment in Palestine.

Now both Mr. Kenen and Dr. Pollack have also made a point of direct talks. I don't know that direct talks are necessarily a criterion of the interest of anybody in peace. As I recall—and there are lawyers in the audience—the UN Charter itself specifies eight or nine different ways in which parties who have conflicts of interest may attempt to resolve them, and direct negotiations are only one of these ways.

But if there are to be direct talks, then it seems to me that because of the breakdown of law the Palestinian entity has become a fact and these are the people with whom the Israelis ought to talk about a settlement. But the reaction of Israel to this—Premier Golda Meir speaks the mind of Israel—is to say the Palestinians don't exist. And I suggest that whatever may be the long and devious path to any settlement, Golda Meir's route does not lead along that path.

Now, beyond this, I recently came across a statement by Dean Acheson and I conclude my rebuttal by reading it and the commentary made on it by C. L. Sulzberger, who is probably not any more pro-Arab than the newspaper which pays his salary. Mr. Acheson said:

> Israel can't win any more great victories and on their side the Arabs are too weak. The United States will inevitably be the big loser as Russia moves in and takes over this junction point of the three continents, Asia, Africa, and Europe. And part of our trouble is that one can't make terrible mistakes without eventually paying for them.

To this observation, which was a direct quote from Acheson, Sulzberger added:

> This statement refers to Acheson's well-known coolness to the idea of creating Israel at all a gen-

eration ago and to his vigorous criticism of the
Eisenhower-Dulles policy of first alienating Nasser
and then supporting him against Britain and France
in 1956.

My observation is that we are in danger. America
and the West are in danger in the Middle East today
because America and the West have had no policy
worthy either of our values or consistent with our
interests in the area. The trouble has been that all
the great statesmen of the United States, and there's
a long list of them, and it grows every year, are
saying that our unqualified endorsement and support of Zionism and subsequently the State of Israel
in the Middle East was a mistake. But they say it
after they put down the tools and the accessories
of power and glory.

ALLEN POLLACK

Mr. Mayhew himself asserted that it was nonsense to talk about a settlement in the Middle East that included the elimination of Israel. I think, therefore, we should not dwell at any great length on Rabbi Berger's assertions of what he would have liked instead of the establishment of the state.

I agree with Mr. Mayhew completely that if there is to be a future for the peoples of the Middle East, it must include a Palestinian entity. I also think the concrete suggestion he made is a viable one in terms of the Palestinian state being primarily the West Bank and Gaza. However, the problem we have is that the only spokesmen of the Palestinian people are just those who will not accept the kind of compromise Mr. Mayhew is advocating. It is a tragedy that the spokesmen for Palestinian nationalism are the guerrilla forces which include as their minimal demand the dissolution of the State of Israel. When the time comes that Palestinian nationalism is represented by people ready to compromise maximalist territorial ambitions for the sake of achieving national self-determination, then perhaps you can have that viable settlement.

Mr. Mayhew stresses that Israel's primary interest is security. That I think is Israel's secondary interest; Israel's primary interest in the Middle East is peace. The Arabs are not ready for peace. Since Israel cannot have peace, it insists on security. Now this is the heart of the matter. For example, if the Arabs would say, "We are ready to live in peace," I think Israel's territorial demands would be quite different from the demands which they must now present—faced as they are with the reaffirmation by the Arab states of their Khartoum principles: no direct negotiations with Israel, no recognition of Israel, and no peace treaty with Israel. These are not the affirmations of people who are ready to live in peace. This is the dilemma that Israel faces.

It's also the dilemma underlying the UN resolution of the Security Council of November 22, 1967. Israel reads the resolution, as did its sponsors, to mean that all of the specifics—territory, Jerusalem, a meaningful settlement of the refugee problem—all of these are attempts to resolve the specific problems as a step toward ultimate peace in the Middle East. The Arabs read the resolution as a way in which they can get back the territory they lost in the war of 1967.

I was somewhat surprised by Mr. Mayhew's written statement to the effect that if only Israel would agree to the Arab interpretation of the UN resolution as meaning complete withdrawal from all territory occupied in 1967, then everything else would be attainable— peace treaties, et cetera, et cetera. It might be easy for Mr. Mayhew to offer peace treaties, but it will not be easy for the Arab states.

The assertion that complete withdrawal from occupied territory is the key to peace is a very interesting one; it makes a very good debating point. But there was a previous war, in 1956—and, as a result of that war, Israel withdrew from every inch of territory it had occupied. That did not lead to peace.

This is one of the reasons why Israel is not willing to say it will withdraw completely now and hopefully accept Mr. Mayhew's assertions that withdrawal will lead to settlement.

I would say the same thing holds true for his great dream of the return of the British and French to the Middle East through the guise of a UN force there. Unfortunately, the United Nations can play—in many areas of the world, certainly in the Middle East—only a very limited role. If the two sides are ready to reach an agreement, you will not need the British, the French, or any other international force to bring them together. And if the two sides are not ready to live in peace, no army the United Nations can amass is strong enough to make them do so. This is why Israel demands security, until the Arabs say: "We are ready to live in peace with a sovereign State of Israel."

The role of the Soviet Union is not as complex or as contradictory as Mr. Mayhew seems to outline. The parallel he seems to draw in terms of the danger of a possible U.S. involvement in the Middle East, similar to our involvement in Vietnam, is misdrawn. The Great Power that is in danger of repeating a "Vietnam" is the Soviet Union. It is facing the problems that the United States faced several years ago—of being drawn into a local war in which its public prestige is committed more and more in support of its client state until it has its own personnel directly involved.

One of the tasks America must undertake for the peace of the world is to keep the Soviet Union from getting as deeply involved in the Middle East as we were in Vietnam. We have to be realistic about the present situation. This presupposes, and this demands, that the United States act to limit the involvement of the Soviet Union and stabilize the situation between Israel and the Arab states until that time comes when the Arabs are ready for peace.

Let me conclude by making one point about a peace treaty. Peace is not a piece of paper; it's a state of mind. I think Israel's insistence on a peace treaty is valid because of what it means for the Arabs. It would be public admission that their opposition to the State of Israel and support for the elimination of the State of Israel had changed. Such public admission, I think, would be the beginning of a process of real change that could ultimately lead to peace.

A peace treaty itself is no security. But a peace treaty would be indication of a change of policy. That is what Israel is looking for. That is what the Arab states have not yet been ready to offer.

CHRISTOPHER MAYHEW

Throughout Dr. Pollack's rebuttal he talked about the Arabs without any discrimination at all, and I do hope very much we won't fall into this trap. As I think I was the first to state: the Palestinians are not willing to have peace except on the basis of a united multi-racial Palestine, which means the dismantling of Israel. That is not true of the Arab governments immediately concerned; and it is certainly not true of President Nasser who consistently has upheld, publicly and privately, the UN Security Council resolution which involves him in accepting the State of Israel and ending the state of belligerency. Indeed, his acceptance of the Rogers proposals—which has exposed him to bitter attack from many other quarters because he was in fact accepting the existence of Israel—surely is proof enough that there are Arabs and there are Arabs.

I would beg our Zionist proponents to believe that the way to peace is to try to help and encourage the more moderate sections in the enemy camp. The effect of the intransigence of Israel's bid is to make the position of President Nasser, King Hussein and others who have stood for the Security Council resolution, who have stood for a deal, more and more difficult. If they go under, if the moderate Arabs go under, it will be because what they have suggested—namely, a deal—has shown no return at all.

Of course it's true, as I was saying, that Israel wants security. But let us be very careful. Let the Israelis be careful not to make people feel that what they want is to be left in peace like a burglar with his loot. Because this is how it appears. If you say we must have peace first and then we'll talk about a Palestinian state, then we'll talk about withdrawal, but first we must have peace, first you must come to direct talks with us, first you must show you have changed your minds and then maybe something will happen—well, if you say this, it is not statesmanship at all.

In the first place, direct talks are very difficult. In the war—in 1940—the French had the same dilemma. Should they talk peace with Hitler while he still occupied northern France? As we know, some Frenchmen said yes. Petain said yes. And some Frenchmen said no. De Gaulle said no. And it's no good asking President Nasser to play the role of Petain and Laval. It's natural that the Israelis should say, first we want acceptance, first we want what we want. And then, I think, it's also natural for some Arabs to say, as they do, first we want withdrawal and then perhaps we'll accept Israel. But we here know that a bargain must be a bargain in which both things happen.

Now, finally, I hope I made clear that the Palestinians are full of violent and passionate feelings. The dreadful truth is that the Jews have now displaced the Palestinians from Palestine much as the Romans dispersed the Jews from Palestine 2,000 years ago. And there is every indication that the Palestinian Arab reaction will be as passionate and as enduring as the Jewish reaction—and that 2,000 years from now, if they don't get back before, the Palestinians will be continuing their claim as the Jews continued their claim. "Palestine is ours. Tomorrow in Jerusalem." They are passionate. Heaven forbid that I should try to say anything else. And the fact that they were there more recently, the fact that their title to their homes and lands is a great deal easier to defend than the title of the Jews—that I think will lead us to mounting difficulty.

With respect to the Soviet bombers, the Soviet Union delivered 12 rather old bombers to the Egyptian government a long time ago. I was saying that it did not deliver either missiles or modern bombers, which it could have done and which would have enabled the Egyptians to bomb Tel Aviv. This contrasts with the attitude of the United States which has given Israel the Phantoms, the first offensive weapons in the Middle East, to enable her to bomb Cairo. Indeed, on the whole subject of armaments, I would ask an American audience to reflect that, since 1948, Israel has been militarily dominant in the region. Everyone agrees with this— the Arabs and the Israelis. That is to say that your arms

deliveries to Israel—so far from establishing a balance
—have increased the military dominance of one party.
The Soviet deliveries to the Arab world have been in
the direction of striking a balance of power there.

Finally, on behalf of my partner Dr. Berger, just let
me say this: He is well known in the Arab world. And
he is a living proof to the Arabs that their opponent,
their enemy, is not the Jewish people, but the Zionists.
He is a living proof, if you like, that there are good
guys as well as bad guys among the Jewish people. And,
for that reason if for no other, when the time comes,
when the dust settles on all this bitter controversy, the
Jewish people will have cause to be grateful to Dr.
Berger.

DISCUSSION

JAMES L. YUENGER, *Chicago Tribune* Press Service: I'd like to make a brief observation and then ask the same question of all the four panelists: Mr. Kenen said that goodwill is required for a Middle East peace and gave no evidence that he believes any exists. Rabbi Berger spoke of a cynical pessimism for a Middle East peace, which seems to bespeak his own attitude, and then he referred to the Middle East as the world's most intractable problem. Dr. Pollack concluded for various reasons that peace is possible in the Middle East, but that when it will come he doesn't know. And Mr. Mayhew, after suggesting specific security guarantees for Israel with the creation of a Palestinian state, said that he considers a settlement unlikely in the foreseeable future.

But this is supposed to be a rational debate with the title, "How Can a Just Peace in the Middle East be Achieved?" We all know that some flexibility is required for peace in the Middle East, and I would like to ask each of the panelists whether they detected in the remarks of the other panelists anything which would provide the kind of flexibility that is required.

PROFESSOR POLLACK: The answer is no, but completely immaterial. With all due respect to Mr.

Mayhew—supposing we reach a compromise on the extent of the Palestinian state—and to Rabbi Berger and Mr. Kenen—supposing we reach another compromise on what the Jewish content of the State of Israel should be—I ask you very frankly: What has that got to do with what's going to happen in the Middle East? If I truly believed that Egypt was as ready publicly to give acceptance to the State of Israel as Mr. Mayhew believes on the basis of his conversations with Nasser, I would be most optimistic. Unfortunately, the world has suffered from President Nasser and King Hussein making excellent statements in England, France, and the United States about their peaceful intentions, and then telling their own people something different. The day Nasser goes on Radio Cairo and delivers the same text that is printed in New York, I will be much more optimistic about his readiness to reach a settlement. I do not know why our government is so ready to accept what some of these Arabs say privately about how they really feel rather than what they say publicly to their own people.

One of the problems in the Middle East has been the growth of extremism, publicly enunciated by both sides. Public statements have contributed to this. When the Arabs are ready to say publicly that their policy of 20 years of opposition to the State of Israel is wrong —or rather has failed—and that they are ready to change it, that would be a sign of flexibility leading to a settlement. But I would conclude by saying that as long as they publicly announce the Khartoum principles as still valid—no direct negotiations, no peace treaty, no recognition of Israel—that is not a sign of the kind of change in their attitude to Israel which peace presupposes.

MR. MAYHEW: Well, I had some flickering hopes during Mr. Kenen's and Dr. Pollack's speeches which I thought were a little bit more flexible than their papers. I think there were one or two bows towards the idea of an independent Palestinian state in the present occupied territories, and that seemed to me something that would be worth perhaps discussing and trying to build on. But then the final remarks of Mr. Kenen set me back again, because here you have this appalling suspiciousness. In fact, Nasser by his words and deeds has committed himself very, very strongly and irrevocably to the Security Council resolution. But that's not good enough for Mr. Kenen. Nasser doesn't mean it; it's a trap. Now that is an attitude of obsessive suspicion.

I have met Mr. Nasser some six or seven times in recent years, I know him very well, and I know what I'm saying is true—that he's willing to give peace a chance. But I know also that there are people like Mr. Kenen whose suspicions are so great that they won't take a chance.

If I could just end by saying this: Everybody can understand, as I said, how deeply sensitive the Israelis feel about security. They are pathologically concerned with their suspicions—with their insecurity. And we know—it's true of people, it's true of individuals—that those who are most insecure are often also the most aggressive. They simply have to dominate their neighbors through fear. And Israel has in fact in recent years relied on military power, relied on the idea of dominating her neighbors—not I think because she's so aggressive, but precisely because she's so pathologically insecure and so unreasonably, so exaggeratedly suspicious. I only hope and pray that, one day, Mr. Kenen will see that a really courageous effort to believe that one Arab leader means what he says might lead to some good.

MR. KENEN: I happen to believe that President Nasser does mean what he says, and he says it very often, he says it very clearly. He told the Egyptian National Assembly in January 1969, with reference to the UN resolution:

> We appreciate the attitude of the Palestinian resistance organizations in rejecting the resolution that was accepted by the U.A.R. They are entitled to reject this resolution which serves the purposes of eliminating the consequences of the June 1967 aggression, but is inadequate for determining the Palestinian fate.

That doesn't encourage me to place much faith in what President Nasser intends.

I think that if anybody has a right to be suspicious, it's the people who observed what happened after the cease-fire went into effect. You haven't referred to it at all tonight, but there was a brazen violation of the standstill agreement. The Nixon administration has finally conceded that to be true. How can you place much reliance on a change in a balance of power which has been brought about by duplicity on the part of the Soviet Union and the U.A.R.? Everybody knows what has happened, except perhaps our friends here, and I don't see how people can expect the Israelis to accept the situation with complacency and without very deep concern.

If you live completely surrounded by enemies and if you are threatened by the strongest power in the area—that is the Soviet Union—and if you listen to nothing but threats all the time over your radio, you will certainly become concerned about your security. And I suspect that the people of Israel in 1967 did believe that many of them—I know this to be true— would die in the war that was being threatened by their neighbors. The Israelis won that war, fortunately. What will happen in the future I do not know, but under the present circumstances I don't think they can place much confidence in their neighbors at this time.

RABBI BERGER: I think too much is made about the difference between what Nasser says to his people and what he says publicly. As I see the press reports from the Middle East, it was no secret to the Egyptian people that after considerable struggle within their own government as there was in Israel, Egypt agreed to the Rogers proposals. But it is true that when Nasser speaks publicly, that is, for the world and to his own people, he always says, "Peace but—." He said this—I think it was on the 27th of May 1967. The "but" involves the points which I have tried, perhaps too academically, to make here tonight.

When you say make peace with Israel, the question still remains: What kind of an Israel? Is it an Israel for the people who are now there, or is it an Israel which 15 years from now may take in all the Jews from the Soviet Union? Combine the open-end arrangement of this Jewish people nationality concept of Zionism with the permissiveness which has operated in Israel's favor to the constant extension of its boundaries, and you have what's really in the back of the minds of the Arab people—fear of a constantly expanding entity in their midst. So I believe that there is—or there was— a chance for peace with the acceptance of the Rogers proposals. What will happen as a result of the last couple of days of course is anyone's guess.

WILLIAM KINTNER, University of Pennsylvania: There has been a great debate for many years about offensive and defensive weapons. There was one at the time of the Cuban missile crisis, for example. It seems to me that if we look at the arms shipments into the Middle East in the past three years that the U.S. contribution has been relatively negligble. The Soviets have supplied a great many tanks; they have supplied artillery, including some very long-range artillery. They are supplying amphibious equipment which I think is destined to cross the depths. Isn't it possible, with this type of equipment, to upset the balance of power around the canal? And isn't it possible that the Soviet Union might be trying to use this situation to gain a dominant position in the Middle East which might in the long run be disastrous to the entire Western position as well as to Israel itself?

MR. MAYHEW: Well, if you take the Suez Canal, is an Egyptian weapon like a tank or an amphibious ship which can cross the canal—is that aggressive or not? I mean—the canal is Egyptian. I read about missiles in the American press as though the missiles were somehow an offensive weapon. But I was in Cairo in January when it was being bombed by your Phantoms. The missiles were a despairing effort to protect the capital of Egypt from Israeli bombing by American planes. Now that is defensive. If anything in the world is defensive it's the Sam-3s and the SAM-2s, and if anything in the world is offensive, it is a Phantom bomber which bombs Cairo. It is a great pity one doesn't see media in this country, if I may say so.

PROFESSOR POLLACK: I think we should realize that the whole question of what's offensive and what's defensive depends very much on the military situation at the time. I sympathize greatly with the people of Cairo who suffered from bombing in their own midst, but the only reason why Israel used Phantoms to begin with was that President Nasser unilaterally ended the cease-fire which was instituted in 1967 and began his self-proclaimed war of attrition. Now, given the nature of facts in the Middle East, Egypt had an overwhelming preponderance of artillery and manpower at the Suez Canal. The only answer that Israel has had for that situation was its planes. So Israel went and bombed with its planes, and Egypt suffered while trying to shoot the planes down. The question to ask is why did Egypt start the war of attrition in 1968.

One of the things Mr. Mayhew mentioned in his paper was that Nasser's acceptance of the Rogers proposals was no change of policy. If there was no change of policy, there would not have had to be a cease-fire along the Suez Canal, because a cease-fire was instituted at the end of the six-day war. One of Israel's points, and the United States theoretically agrees, is that the cease-fire instituted in 1967 is still supposed to be in effect. Nasser broke it; Nasser suffered the consequences; and then Nasser went to Moscow to ask the Russians to help figure out a way for him to escape the consequences of his unilateral action.

RABBI RICHARD HIRSCH, Union of American Hebrew Congregations: I want to ask two questions, basically of Mr. Mayhew. I understand that you delineate between two groups—the moderate Arab states and the Palestinians—and that your two proposals are made to meet the needs of each of these groups. As for the first group, the moderate Arab states, you claim that their basic concern is to regain their territory. You say, how can you expect them to live in peace "with a burglar who has the loot"? The question is: on June 4,

1967 there was no burglar, there was no loot. What elements pertained? Why would the Arabs now accept peace, when on June 4 they had the territory that you suggest now be returned to them?

My second question deals with the Palestinians. You say that the Palestinian state if such a state were created, would give self-determination to the Palestinians—it would let off the steam and that there would therefore be peace. I personally happen to agree with you.

I think there is much merit in the idea of a Palestinian entity. But I have several questions that I'd like to ask you. Why was there no talk of a Palestinian state on the West Bank between 1948 and 1967 when the Arabs had complete control of both territories and ideology? Why was there no comment from the Palestinians when Jordan annexed the West Bank? And why is there no comment now on a Palestinian state from any organized Palestinian group—either on the West Bank or in Jordan? As far as I know, the only discussion presently going on within the area of Palestine and Israel about a Palestinian state exists in the State of Israel. Why you can hardly pick up a magazine or a newspaper which does not have an article about the so-called Palestinian entity.

MR. MAYHEW: On the second point first, I think we have to recognize that the Palestinians were knocked out for 20 years after 1948. They were in the camps, they were dispersed, they had no—they were knocked

out. They were no political force really until about 1957
or 1958. I can only say that.

But now they have recovered their poise, their sense
of national consciousness, and this does present a real
problem. And no solution will be viable in my judgment unless some concession is made to their aspirations.
If you ask why is there so little talk of what I was
saying, I really believe it's because this idea is still—
as far as the Arabs in the West are concerned anyhow
—a fresh one.

On your first question about 1967, it assumes that
the Arabs started the war in 1967. Now this is the
assumption made throughout the length and breadth
of the United States, as though it were—you know—
established. People don't even discuss it. All I can assure
you of is this: to the extent that the assumption prevails
in the United States, you are simply isolating yourselves
from the main trend of world opinion and from historical fact.

JAMES SAMS, Attorney, Washington, D.C.: I would
like Mr. Kenen and Dr. Pollack to comment on this
observation. They appeared to emphasize that the dispute must be resolved by the parties themselves in direct
negotiation. I guess they are proceeding upon the
premise that the parties are Israel and the Arab states of
Jordan and Egypt, perhaps Syria, Lebanon, and Iraq.
There is no reference to the Palestinians as a party.
Second, there is no reference to the fact that neither
the Israelis nor any of the Arab states, nor the Pales-

tinians, could possibly hope to implement any of their policies without support from external forces, principally the United States and the Soviet Union. So it seems difficult to me to challenge the need for external direct involvement in any solution for the area. I'm a little concerned that in a discussion of approaches to peace we are concentrating on the same basic arguments, or the positions taken by the various parties, when it seems to me that any real approach would have to involve a thorough discussion of what the United States is going to do, or could or should do, and what the Soviet Union could or should do.

PROFESSOR POLLACK: There are two components to the problem. First, the outstanding issues between Israel and the Arab states have to be resolved by Israel and the Arab states; the issues between Israel and the Palestinians have to be resolved by Israel and the Palestinians. Second, the Great Powers must get involved, but they can only settle the issues between *them*. Specifically, what I'm saying is that the United States and Russia must talk—I'm all in favor of two-power talks. The only problem is they're talking about the wrong things. America and Russia can't force a settlement between Israel and the Arab states that will be lasting. They tried to do that in 1957 and you had another war. Only Israel and the Arab states can reach a meaningful settlement between them.

The Great Powers should be discussing how to make sure that they will not be involved in any further confrontation. And they should be involved perhaps even in a limitation of armaments. One of the reasons for the escalation is that Israel insists on more modern weapons because the Arabs get more modern weapons from Russia.

I think you have to stabilize the situation between the Great Powers so that the danger to the world is avoided. That done, the only meaningful settlement between the nations in the Middle East must come from the Middle East. Moscow and Washington might reach complete agreement on what they think the Mideast frontiers should be, but unless the peoples of the Middle East are ready to accept such an agreement, it is not going to last.

HERBERT FIERST, Attorney, Washington, D.C.: Mr. Mayhew, you propose a demilitarized zone on both sides of the old pre-1967 frontier, perhaps averaging about 30 kilometers and manned by a UN peace-keeping force including sizable French and British contingents. If I might borrow some British understatement, this seems to me preposterously impractical. Number one: it would blanket all parts of Israel, for example, the entire upper Galilee and a substantial part of the Mediterranean coast. Number two: it would not provide Israel with any protection against terrorist attacks. And number three: based on rather intimate past experience, it is most unlikely that Israel would accept sizable or unsizable contingents from either the United Kingdom or France in any of the peace-keeping forces.

MR. MAYHEW: First, I meant 15 kilometers one way and 15 the other on the average. There are obviously parts of the frontier where it doesn't make sense, I agree. I only said an average of 30 kilometers. And when you take 15 kilometers back from the Israeli side it doesn't have the effect, if I may say so, which you outline. Second, you say it wouldn't stop the terrorist attacks. But would the terrorist attacks be stopped by not having a demilitarized zone—by having nothing between the Palestinian state and Israel? It stands to reason that to have a demilitarized zone with the United Nations enforcing it would at least lessen the chances of having terrorist attacks.

Third, you say the Israelis will not accept the French and the British. You may well be right. They won't accept a great deal, I'm afraid, of this conception. They won't, at the moment, accept withdrawal to lines with insubstantial changes as suggested in the Rogers proposal. What I ask the Israelis is: "What is your alternative? If you don't want a UN force with the French and the British there, do you really want a single frontier between yourselves and the Arabs?"

I mean, I just don't see this. I quite agree the Israelis are not responding, and I spoke to Mr. Eban himself about the ideas I put forth tonight, just as in confidence I spoke to President Nasser and King Hussein about them. President Nasser said, "Well, it's easier for us to accept the French than the British." But after considering it with his foreign minister, he added, "If this were part of a package deal, we would present it—though it has neocolonial overtones we don't like—as a safe-guard to our own peoples against further Israeli expansion. And it would be all right with us."

When I spoke to Mr. Eban about it, he simply showed that he was not really concerned with Israel's security on her own frontiers. And, indeed, I established at that time—in Israel earlier this year—that the Israeli chiefs of staff had actually not even been asked to make an appreciation of Israel's security on her old frontiers. So academic was the idea considered to be.

Now, I'm not saying my proposal is perfect. There would still be risks for Israel. But what are the prospects for her now? That's the point. Above all, what are the prospects for her towards the end of the 1970s? Mr. Kenen has just told us he wants the Great Powers to keep out—naturally, because Israel is militarily dominant, because she has the power. And Israel can handle the situation while she remains like that.

But I recall that, in 1967, before it was plain that Israel would dominate, she was begging the Americans and the British to rally round in defense of Israel. And in the end of the 1970s, Mr. Kenen, if the balance of power goes the other way, the Israelis will be coming to the United States, I promise you, and saying, "You've supported us so far but now it's going wrong. We want you in. We want you by our side." And you'll be faced with the dilemma you are faced with in Vietnam—either to let your client go under, having encouraged her by your actions to be intransigent, or else to go in with your own troops and face another and much worse Vietnam.

HARRY N. HOWARD, Adjunct Professor, American University: I have only one question, and I'd like to ask it, really, of Rabbi Berger. Would he comment on two recent articles by Dr. Nahum Goldmann. In an article in *Foreign Affairs* you may recall, Dr. Goldmann made a confession of failure as well as a confession of faith. He said that Israel as a militarist state could not fulfill the Zionist dream or solve the two basic problems of Israel's relations with the Arabs and with the Jews of the Diaspora. In a second article the *New Outlook* of Tel Aviv, he called upon Israel, the Israeli government, to abandon its rigid policy—its rigid attitude—and adopt a much more flexible policy toward the problem of peace in that area.

RABBI BERGER: I think the whole Goldmann episode is one of the most fascinating and, unfortunately in my judgment, least probed developments in this problem, certainly in the last three years. Ideologically, Nahum Goldmann and I are 180 degrees apart. And, therefore, it's very significant, I think, that this man who has spent his whole life in the Zionist movement, who is certainly one of the architects of the State of Israel, has decided that the policies this state and the Zionist movement have pursued are leading down a blind alley. I don't know whether there's any substance to his report that there was a possibility of his going to

Cairo or not. But it is very revealing that it was the
Israeli government which spilled the beans about this
and killed whatever chance there was—assuming there
was any such invitation. It is also, in my judgment, very
interesting that it is Israel which has been, for the most
part, free of the protests we have seen throughout the
rest of the world. The whole revelation—disclosure—
that there was the possibility of some progress being
made through the whole Goldmann approach, and then
the flat way in which the Israeli government just killed
the thing, instigated one of the first at least reportable
protests to the rest of the world that has ever occurred
in Israel. I'm inclined to agree with Goldmann's judgments about the present situation.

PROFESSOR W. T. MALLISON, JR., The George
Washington University Law Center: I would like to
ask Dr. Pollack and Rabbi Berger to comment on the
general theme of what kind of a State of Israel the
United States is supposed to support. More specifically,
is it in our interest to support a Zionist state for the
Jewish people which has very definite self-segregated
aspects—including a nationality law, the "law of
return," which solicits Jewish immigration from all
over the world but makes it legally impossible for a
Palestinian born in the country to return? Are we
interested in supporting that kind of state or should
there be changes in the State of Israel which would
make it more consistent with American values and a
more likely bet for peace in the Middle East?

PROFESSOR POLLACK: The State of Israel that I want the United States to support is a state that determines its own policies. As far as the "law of return" is concerned, it offers a Jew anywhere in the world the right to come to Israel. I think that's a provision that must be maintained. As for Israel not letting a Palestinian who is born in that area come back, I truly expect that the day after peace is signed between Israel and a Palestinian state, there will be free trade and free access and free movement of population. But to ask a state, any state in the world, to welcome home people dedicated to its destruction is unthinkable.

As for what the United States should do, it should support Israel, not for the interests of the Jewish people, but because America has vital interests in the Middle East which Israel is protecting.

RABBI BERGER: I think that I've touched on my ideas about this. I do not agree with the whole Zionist concept that anti-Semitism is endemic and incurable and, therefore, there has to be a State of Israel to which any Jew can go. This may be all right provided it's not done at the expense of people who have rights in the country to which these Jews are being invited from all over the world. One of the things the American people ought to know is that at this moment funds which are being raised in the United States—so-called charitable funds—are supporting ten regional offices recruiting American Jews to go to Israel. And I really don't see that kind of anti-Semitism in the United

States today. I think the United States, both by virtue
of what we believe to be American values and by virtue
of the laws of the United States, could make some contribution to a peace settlement—a stabilization of the
Middle East—by requiring some regularizing of the
Zionist operation in the United States.

NOTES

FIRST LECTURE

[1] Dag Hammarskjold, UN Secretary General.

SECOND LECTURE

[1] Philip L. Geyelin and Douglass Cater, *American Media: Adequate or Not?* (Washington: American Enterprise Institute, 1970).

[2] The date of this agreement was January 3, 1919. Among forgotten stipulations is the pledge, in Article V, that "No religious test shall ever be required for the exercise of civil or political rights." But the most important of the "neglected" items was the "Reservation by the Emir Faisal" which stipulated, for the Arabs, that the agreement would be valid only if Arab aspirations for independence and self-determination were realized. It was this reservation which for a long time was omitted from widely publicized versions of the agreement. The extensive circulation by the Zionists was to create the impression that "the Arabs" welcomed the Zionist activity in Palestine, without any serious questions whatsoever. For the text of the agreement, see Walter Laquer, ed., *The Israel-Arab Reader* (New York: Bantam Books, 1969), p. 18.

[3] Fred J. Khouri, *The Arab/Israeli Dilemma* (Syracuse, N.Y.: Syracuse University Press, 1968), p. 10.

[4] See, for example, Department of State, *Foreign Relations of the United States, 1944*, Vol. V (Washington, D.C.: Government Printing Office), pp. 560-660; also, same series, Vol. VIII for 1945, pp. 678-844. See also George Lenczowski, *The Middle East in World Affairs*, second edition (Ithaca, New York: Cornell University Press, 1956), p. 350; Walter Millis, ed., *The Forrestal Diaries* (New York: The Viking Press, 1951), pp. 347, 348, 357, 360-61, 363, and 371.

[5] Alan R. Taylor, *Prelude to Israel* (Beirut: The Institute for Palestine Studies, 1970), p. 53.

[6] Nahum Goldmann, *The Autobiography of Nahum Goldmann* (New York: Holt, Rinehart and Winston, 1969), p. 285.

[7] Khouri, *op. cit.*, p. 293.

[8] General Assembly Resolution 273 (III), May 11, 1949.

[9] Khouri, *op. cit.*, pp. 106-07.

[10] Jacob L. Talmon, "History as Fixation and Guide," *To Make War or Make Peace*, Symposium on the Middle East (Tel Aviv: New Outlook, 1969), p. 50.

[11] E. L. Woodward and Rohan Butler, editors, *Documents on British Foreign Policy, 1919-1939* (London: H.M. Stationery Office, 1952), p. 345.

[12] Harry N. Howard, *The King-Crane Commission* (Beirut: Khayats, 1963), p. 311.

[13] The quoted language, here and immediately following, is from the Balfour Declaration.

[14] For a legal analysis see, W. T. Mallison, Jr., "The Zionist-Israel Juridical Claims to Constitute 'the Jewish People' Nationality Entity and to Confer Membership In It: Appraised in Public International Law," *The George Washington Law Review,* Vol. 32, June 1964, No. 5, Washington, D.C.

[15] *Ibid.,* p. 1005.

[16] See the numerous references in any edition of Theodor Herzl's *The Jewish State,* or any edition of Herzl's Diaries.

[17] Fayez A. Sayegh, "A Palestinian View," *Time Bomb in the Middle East* (New York: Friendship Press, 1969), p. 48.

[18] Leonard Stein, *The Balfour Declaration* (London: Vallentine-Mitchell, 1961), pp. 418, 524.

[19] Theodore Herzl, founder and first president of the World Zionist Organization.

[20] Quoted from a New York Yiddish newspaper, *Der Yid,* of June 25, 1965, in Emile Marmorstein, *Heaven at Bay* (London: Oxford University Press, 1969), p. 79. See also, the memorandum from Allen Dulles, Director, Division of Near Eastern Affairs, United States Department of State, to the assistant secretary and the under secretary of state, May 2, 1922, The National Archives, Washington, D.C., Record Group No. 59, Index Bureau 867 N. 01/214.

[21] The language is from the Israeli courts and was used in the judgment of the Eichmann trial (Criminal Case No. 40/61, District Court of Jerusalem, Par. 34.)

[22] See *Foreign Relations of the United States,* 1945, Vol. VIII, *op. cit.,* p. 698.

[23] David Nevin, "Autocrat in the Action Arena," *Life,* September 5, 1969, p. 50B.

[24] Lawrence Mosher, "Zionist Role in U.S. Raises New Concern," *The National Observer,* May 18, 1970, p. 1.

[25] *The Christian Science Monitor,* July 25, 1970, p. 11.

[26] UN General Assembly Resolution, 2535 (XXIV), December 10, 1969.

[27] See, for example, the confused—and confusing—rulings by the Department of State and the Department of Justice on Afroyim v. Rusk, 387 U.S. 253 (1967), "Opinion of the Attorney General of the United States," January 18, 1969, and "Statement on Foreign Military Service of U.S. Citizens," Robert McCloskey (Department of State), October 18, 1969.

[28] See particularly paragraphs 5 and 6 of the "World Zionist Organization/ Jewish Agency (Status) Law, 5713-1952" in *Fundamental Laws of the State of Israel,* edited by Joseph Badi, Twayne, New York, 1961, p. 285.

[29] *Jewish Agency Digest,* Jerusalem, May 16, 1952, pp. 1069-70.

[30] The best recent expose of the intricate fund-raising of the Zionists in the United States, is the article in *The National Observer* by Lawrence Mosher. See *supra* note 24. For a more detailed and official disclosure see *Hearing,* "Activities of Nondiplomatic Representatives of Foreign Principals in the

United States," Parts 9 and 12, May 23 and August 1, 1963, United States
Government Printing Office, Washington, 1963.

[31] Jewish Telegraphic Agency report in *The Jewish News*, Newark, N.J., July 17,
1970, p. 6. In September of 1970 there were 12 recruiting centers in the
United States and Canada. On September 9 the President of the Synagogue
Council of America issued an appeal to American rabbis to include an appeal
for immigration to Israel in their sermons for the Jewish High Holy days.

[32] *Reports*, Submitted to the Twenty-Seventh Zionist Congress in Jerusalem,
Jewish Agency, Jerusalem, May 1968, p. 52.

[33] *Ibid.*, p. 87.

[34] *Statement for the Record*, prepared for the Near East Subcommittee, Committee
on Foreign Affairs, House of Representatives, Dr. W. T. Mallison, Jr. (Submitted August 21, 1970). This statement will be published as a part of the
record of the hearings held in July of 1970 by this subcommittee, p. 11.

[35] Authoritative reports in August 1970 stated that the Israeli government
planned, with the Jewish Agency, to raise $1 billion in 1971 "for its non-
defense needs." Israel's finance minister stated that "defense costs [were]
absorbing 85% of Israel's budget ($1.45 billion, four times greater than in
1966). Israel is no longer able to provide its citizens and new immigrants
with necessary social services." (Jewish Telegraphic Agency dispatch, Jerusalem,
in *The Jewish News*, Newark, N.J., September 4, 1970, p. 2.) If the campaign
for this amount conforms to previous patterns, somewhere between 70 percent
and 80 percent of this goal will be expected from "tax-deductible" U.S. funds.

[36] Uri Davis, *The Middle East Paper*, Prepared for War Resisters International
Conference, Haverford, Pennsylvania, August 1969.